© Patrick Cronin 2017

Front Cover: Custom House Quay, Greenock Harbour
Illustration by Ellie Cronin ©2017

Contents

Acknowledgements	3
Introduction	5
Preparing for the Voyage	6
The Hero	10
The Diary	11
The Shenir	15
29th October – Collision at Sea	68
British Passengers Act Extract	92
Great Sandy Island	114
The Liechardt	121
Maryborough Harbour	123
Gympie	129
Robert Rankine	131
Obituary of William Rankine	134
Index to Passengers	138
William Rankines Family Tree	153
Jim Thomson Family Tree	154
Extended Family	155

Acknowledgements

There are several people and institutions I wish to thank for their assistance in finalising this project without which this publication would never have been completed.

Thanks go to Rosemary Phillis, Secretary at Riverstone and District Historical Society Inc., who so generously and enthusiastically sourced and provided several family photographs, newspaper cuttings and related records – these help greatly in bringing the diary to life.

Thanks also to Jean Singleton of Live Borders, Chambers Institution in Peebles for locating William Rankines place of death and pointing me to several locations in Peebles associated with the Rankine family.

I am grateful to The State Records Authority of New South Wales for the passenger list.

Finally sincere thanks to my daughter Ellie for her artwork and her digital imaging skills, and for her assistance with the book design, and to my son Aidan for his music notation skills.

Patrick Cronin,

Fountainstown, County Cork

July 2017

From Peebles to Gympie

The Diary of William Rankine

Narrative & Transcription by Patrick Cronin

Introduction

In September 1882, more than four hundred souls set out for the long voyage to Queensland, New South Wales. This is the diary of one of those passengers, William Rankine, great great uncle to my wife Christine, who inherited the diary from her father William McInally. The diary records[2] the detail of the voyage from Scotland, and presents a rare first hand record of the adventure, hardships, monotony and dangers encountered by ordinary people as they set sail into a new world. Where possible, supporting

---

[1] Photo Courtesy of Riverstone and District Historical Society
[2] Spelling and grammar are faithful to the original text, and no attempt has been made to correct inconsistencies.

documents, drawings, photographs and contemporary news reports have been sourced and included in this transcript, to enhance the readers understanding of Williams's journey.

William was born in Peebles in 1861 to Robert Rankine and Jane Melrose. His father Robert, a joiner by trade, was very likely a member of the local masonic lodge, since Robert and Jane lived for a time at No.9 Northgate, Peebles which was the home of the lodge from 1716. Prior to emigrating William lived all of his years in Peebles at his parents address in Damdale. He was strictly Presbyterian. By 1881 he appears in the census records as a plumber. In 1882 he decided to emigrate to Queensland, Australia, and booked his passage under the Governments Assisted Package scheme.

Preparing for the Voyage

It is quite possible that, before his travels William had read the 1860s publication titled "Out at Sea or The Emigrant Afloat"[3] which was described as a "hand book of practical information for the use of passengers on a long sea voyage". This handbook included all manner of useful information for the traveller, including a discussion on the time of year to travel, and what to consider when choosing a company to travel with, to a list of necessities to

---

[3] Written by P.B.Chadfield of Chadfield & Son, Printers of Derby

carry, menus and recipes, and a discussion on social life on board ship.

For example, it suggested the following outfit and provisions would be required:

For each male adult, amongst other things:

"a mattress, 20 inches wide by 6 feet long;

6 shirts, white or coloured;

3 Guernsey or flannel shirts;

6 pairs of stockings, half worsted;

1 pair of good stout shoes;

1 pair of good stout boots;

1 suit of warm outer clothing;

1 suit of light clothing with extra trousers;

1 light cap, 1 warm cap or southwester;

Sheets, blankets, towels, pocket handkerchiefs;

A tin chamber with lid; a slop pail with cover;

A safety lamp for the berth;

4 pounds of soap, yeast, 6 pounds of candles;

Castor oil, aperient pills[4], calomel powders[5];

Ipecacuanha powders[6];

eggs may be kept by smearing them with butter or lard and packing in salt".

Separate lists of clothing were suggested for women and children, and while the handbook recognised

---

[4] To relieve constipation
[5] A mercury based compound used as a laxative
[6] A powdered root purgative/evacuant/laxative

that these suggestions were the ideal, extra provisions should be brought according to means.

Surprisingly the handbook did not go into any significant detail on the rules of behaviour to be followed while at sea, but did recognise the challenge posed by having the different classes of people rubbing shoulders for 3 months in confined quarters. The one bit of advice given was that difficulties on board had to be endured by all and "any display of bad feeling is sure to recoil tenfold on the party exhibiting it". Overall, it is clear that the handbook, though excellent practical advice for all, was written by and for those better off.

William set out on his journey on Thursday, September 21st 1882. What was going through his mind as he stood on the ferry Hero, on what he likely considered his final journey down the Clyde to Glasgow? As a young man it appears he had never travelled far from Peebles, and here he was, setting out to cross the world, leaving all of his family and friends behind. It is clear that he was an educated man, with an interest in all that he could learn from the press about the world at home and abroad, but he could never have fully anticipated the sights and experiences he would encounter over the coming months. He promised his family to dutifully record in his diary everything he saw and heard on the voyage, and to send this diary home when he got the opportunity.

By no means was he the first to embark on such a journey – the opportunities open to young men in 1880s Scotland were few, and in the years before him many thousands set out in search of a better life. Many went west, but several Peebles families had already made the trip to Queensland in search of a better life, and for some the pull of the gold rush in Gympie was strong.

The trip would cost William very little if anything. Most people travelling under the Governments "Assisted Passage" scheme paid nothing at all. This scheme was funded in order to encourage skilled and unskilled labour to emigrate during periods of economic expansion in the colonies. Only time would tell whether the decision to go was right or wrong, and as Williams diary shows, life at sea was precarious especially for steerage passengers in overcrowded, cramped and often filthy conditions.

The Hero[7]

The ferry on which he commenced his voyage had been plying its trade since it had been built by Wingates in 1858. Originally owned by Mr Alexander Watson, it was a paddle steamer and was the first steamer with a flat floor. Its haystack boiler was the first of its type to be built of steel, and its steeple type engine was one of the most successful of its kind. It operated for many years as a ferry between Rothesay and Broomielaw, with a connection to the train from Glasgow at Greenock Quay.

For a time it also steamed between Arran and the Kyles. Unlike the vessel which would transport William to Queensland, the Hero was exempt from

the law relating to the sale of alcohol on Sundays. In 1860 it made the headlines when its Captain and Steward were fined for selling ale while still lying in harbour. Whether William would have known or

---

[7] The Hero, Approx. Dimensions: 181' x 19' x 7'

Subsequently renamed "Mountaineer", it was still operating out of Oban in 1903.

been much concerned with these technical details as he started out we don't know, but he would have been aware of the ferry Hero from daily press timetables.

September 21st 1882, Thursday

At 10a.m. we got aboard the river steamer Hero

which had been chartered to take the emigrants to the Tail of the Bank[8]. I need not describe the journey down the river Clyde. When we reached Greenock Jim Thomson left me, and then I was among strangers. I will never forget his kindness[9] . His was the last Peebles face I saw as he stood waving a last farewell. But I was very fortunate in having James Layton for a mate for he is a very nice fellow. All eyes were now on the look-out for the ship SHENIR which was to be our abode for 2 or 3 months at least. Some of these I heard and saw pointing out various ships which they imagined was the SHENIR but she was lying furthest round of any of them almost in Greenock Bay. After arriving alongside the vessel we had to wait about 2

---

[8] The Tail of the Bank is the name given to the anchorage in the upper Firth of Clyde immediately North of Greenock

[9] James Simpson Thomson, a plumber, who would marry Williams sister Jane, and emigrate to Taree, NSW, in late 1888, photo courtesy of Riverstone and District Historical Society Inc

hours before we got on board owing to the temporary berths not having been finished. When we did get on board there was scarcely moving room. We went downstairs to get out of the bustle and hunted up our berths in each of which was placed our bedding and cooking utensils. Dinner was ordered as soon as we were on board but it was late in the afternoon before we saw food. During this time we were idling on deck till dinner. We had time to look about us and see how we were to be placed. On deck there was fitted up for our convenience a bathroom and 2 WCs. It did not look very comfortable down below – fancy 120 beds placed in a space about 30x50. While we were below the Agent General came down and divided us into messes of 10 persons each, the first name on the list to be Captain of the mess for a week, next man being captain next week and so on. My name is second on the card. His duties are to go to the cookhouse and get the supplies for the mess. There are nine Constables on board. They have a blue gannsey with the word Constable across the breast in red letters. The duties of the Constable are to prevent smoking between decks and to look after the cleanliness of those under his charge. They stay up time about for to keep the lamps burning and see that there is nothing wrong. There is three for each part of the ship. The young womans constable has to take their provisions to them, they get 5 pounds for it. The others get 3 pounds. The young girls are at the stern of the ship and the married people in midships and the single men in the fore part of the ship. We received a visit from the Board of Trade shortly after we arrived. These officers put the crew through lifeboat practice and fired off the signal gun and had a look into all corners but found no fault as far as I could learn. After the visit we got time to take our dinner which consisted of beef and potatoes.

About an hour after we got our dinner the tea was ready. Half a pint of tea each and half a small loaf. Tea being over we again went on deck and amused ourselves as best we could singing and shouting, of course this was among the young men. We never up to this time got a glimpse of the girls at the other end of the ship but we can hear them singing "Hes a Jolly Good Fellow" and such like.

 So after a good nights enjoyment we thought of turning into bed when the tug came alongside bringing the Pilot on board. He had to return to Greenock with 3 of the girls who had turned faint-hearted and thought they would stay at home. Coming straight back to the ship we cast the towline on board and set off about 10p.m. This our first days experience being over we turned into bed about 12p.m.

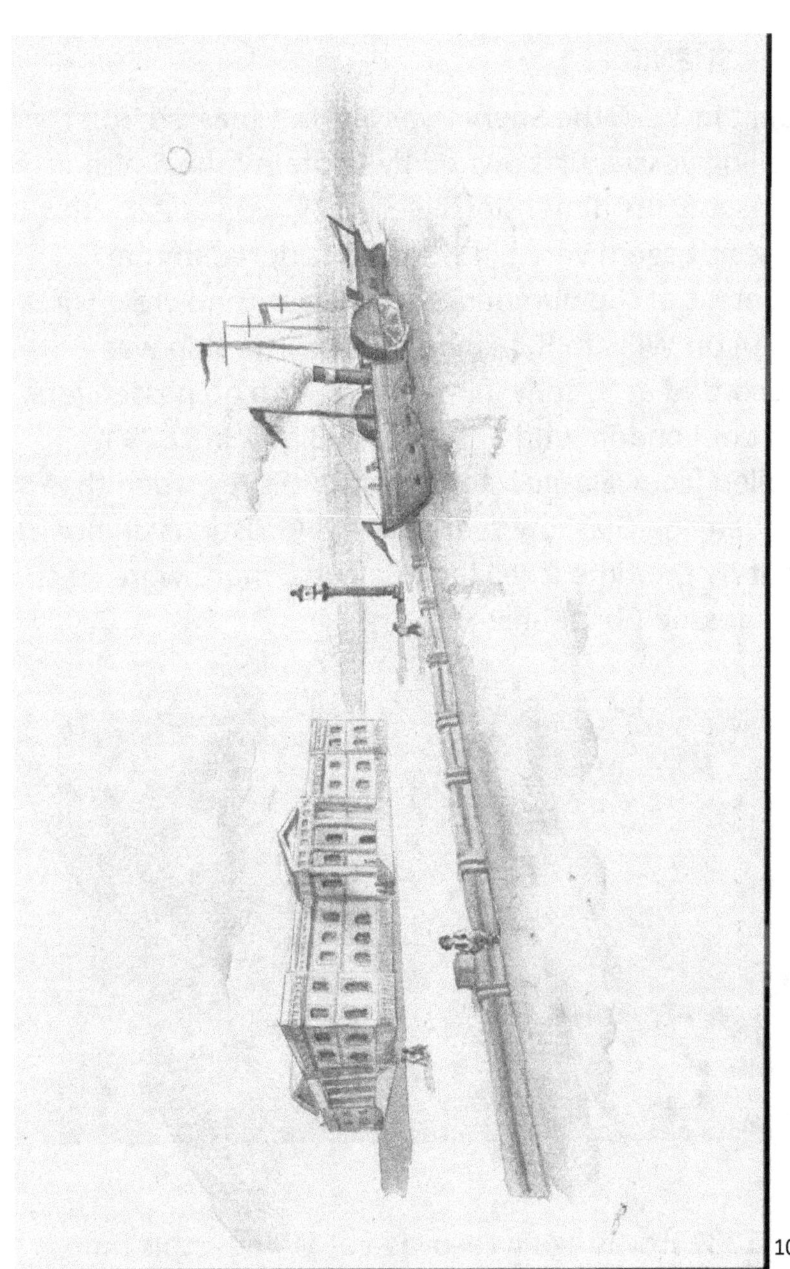

10

---

[10] Greenock Custom House Quay, artwork by Ellie Cronin

The SHENIR

Built in 1876 the Shenir was a three-masted iron sailing vessel, first owned by Captain John Smith of Glasgow. Its dimensions were 225' x 35' x 22' – this doesn't seem very big when considered in the context of the number of passengers and crew (circa 410) on William Rankines voyage. The ship was recorded at Sydney in mid-1878 with no passengers, out of London, under a Captain Black. In 1879 it sailed from Glasgow to Calcutta. It is recorded that on leaving Glasgow there were 8 Christians on board, but by the time it reached Calcutta there were 21 professed Christians.

In 1881 it was again recorded at Sydney, this time out of Liverpool. The Crew & Passenger list is shown here:

---

¹¹ Image from the State Library Victoria, out of copyright:- Brodie Collection, La Trobe Picture Collection, Accession no(s) H99.220/696

No. 1442

Price, 3d.

INWARD.

A LIST of the Crew and Passengers arrived in the Ship *"Shenir"* of Glasgow R. Burthen, 1173 Tons, from the Port of Liverpool to Sydney, New South Wales, 3.

Seamen's Names.	Station.	Age.	Of what Nation.	Names of Passengers.	Description.
John George Liddell	1st Mate	21	British		
Arch.d Campbell	2nd —	20	do	Mrs R. Stirling	
James Cassidy	Carpenter	22	do	Martha Stirling	
William Morton	Boatswain	50	do	John Stirling	
Peter Busbrave	Sailmr	34	do	John Gilroy	Lid. 9/12/81
Aron Olsen	Steward	41	Sweden		
John Mawson	Cook	49	British		
John Corcoran	A.B.	38	do		
Andrew Peterson	A.B.	37	Sweden		
Ingebrigt Storksen	A.B.	27	Bergen		
Demetrius Cavalas	A.B.	31	French		
James Taylor	A.B.	24	British		
Lawrence Lawrence	A.B.	29	do		
Andrew Umphray	A.B.	25	do		
Robt McIndoe	A.B.	26	do		
William Murphy	A.B.	29	do		
George Springfield	A.B.	32	do		
Charle M. Pidgeon	O.S.	19	do		
T. H. Green	O.S.	19	do		
Elijah Farmer	Boy	15	do		
Henry John Popham	Apprentice	16	do		
Reginald Sharp Hawkin	do	17	do		
James Craig	do	19	do		
Charle Hardy	do	16	do		

The Captain was Robert Stirling, and the only passengers on the 1881 voyage were his wife (possibly Annie) and two children, Martha & John, plus one stowaway. Robert Sterling was also Captain for William Rankines passage to Maryborough in 1882, and although he was still Master of the Shenir in 1888, as recorded in another London to Sydney voyage, it seems the crews frequently changed. Although the full crew list for Williams Maryborough trip is not recorded here, it is highly probable that the First Mate was named James McDonald, and the second Mate was Jim Layton; while William named the second purser as Mr.McAllister. The Shenir was still sailing in early 1900[12], was renamed Petra in 1905 and ultimately in December 1910 she was wrecked off Pennant Island, Nova Scotia, on a voyage between Rio de Janeiro and Halifax.

Friday 22nd Sept.

Rose about 4 a.m.to get a look at Ailsa Craig but could just see it in the dark and after a time we saw the north of Ireland and then the pilot got letters to take ashore. Shortly after breakfast the tug left us, as before this we had set all sail and the wind now rising. We were not long in showing the tug the road so the tug cast the towline and we landed it on board and then the tug came alongside and took the Pilot on board so with a shout we bid the tug goodbye it

[12] Lloyds Register 1899/1900.

being the last remnant of Scotland we would see for some time to come. This is a fine day and a splendid wind. We are going about 11 or 12 knots an hour but this tells on some of the young men, nearly two thirds of them are sick. You can see them in nearly every corner and leaning over the side of the ship vomiting. I was only sick for about 5 minutes but felt very strange while at the other end of the vessel I don't see a single young woman. From what I hear they are in a dreadful state. When it came to dinner time there was very few at the tables, a great many of them were in their bunks and some on deck. We have plenty of music on board, one fiddle, 2 concertinas, 3 accordions and one tin whistle. The emigrants subscribed for 1 accordion and 1 concertina before we left so they belong to anybody. We were making 12 knots today. There is a condensing engine on board for supplying us with water.

Saturday Sept. 23rd

Head wind today, making no progress. Before breakfast we hove an empty cask overboard, up till dark it was still in sight. There was a stowaway made his appearance in the afternoon, he had been down in the sail locker till this time. The Mate took him to the Captain who after questioning him for some time gave him a place in the port watch and told him to behave himself. He had been a clerk in G. and S.W. Railway but wanted to get to Queensland. He applied to the Captain for a berth and on being refused took this means of getting a passage.

Who was the stowaway? Typically his name would appear on the passenger list as an addition, and his status would be noted as on the 1881 example above, but no stowaway appears on the Shenir passenger list. His name may have appeared on the crew list since it seems he was put to work. His treatment appears quite civilised, but would be contrary to 20th century guidelines which read "Any stowaways found should be placed in secure quarters, guarded if possible, and be provided with adequate food and water …The Master and crew should act firmly, but humanely….Stowaways should not be put to work. If working, they will be at an increased risk of injuries which may lead to significant medical and deviation expenses". It was only 14 years since, in 1868, the people of Greenock were faced with the horrors that could be experienced by stowaways, when two local boys who had stowed away with 5 others in the ship 'Arran' bound for Quebec, had been abandoned 3 months into the voyage after appalling mistreatment, and perished in horrible circumstances. That case caused outrage across the sailing community, so perhaps informed the manner in which Captain Stirling dealt with stowaways on the Shenir.

Sunday 24th Sept.

We are doing a little better today, we have a favourable bearing and we lost sight of Ireland this morning. A large steamer passed us but I do not know her name or whither bound. She was getting it pretty rough, we could see her propeller sometimes up in the air. We saw some large whales and porpoises sporting in the water. We had religious service on board forenoon and evening conducted by the Salvation Army captain. There is a detachment of the Salvation Army on board going to Queensland. It is a splendid sight but I would rather see it a little rougher as we would then have more wind. We have made very little progress this two days and the little we have made is taking us out of our course. We are in the track of the American steamers and we should be a good deal further south. We passed S.S.Polynesian on her way home and there seemed to be a lot of passengers on it. We gave her three cheers which was returned. Through the carelessness of the man on the lookout she was not reported or we might have got a letter home.

The Polynesian was a passenger ship built in 1872 at Greenock for the Allan Line, and plied its trade sailing between Liverpool and Quebec. She had departed Quebec on or about 3rd September 1882, and a week after William Rankines sighting, she is reported to have departed from Liverpool on 5th October, calling at Londonderry on 6th en route to Quebec once more. Dimensions: 400' x 42'. She was refitted and renamed the Laurentian in 1893, and was used once to transport troops during the Boer War. On 6th September 1909 she was wrecked[13] at Mistaken Point, Trepassey Bay, nr Cape Race, Newfoundland on a Boston to Glasgow run. She was the 20th Allan Line steamer to be lost[14].

On Board

No sooner was William on board than he noted the very little space the passengers had to live in. The arrangement of the accommodation as described by William was the norm, but the numbers obviously varied greatly. On Williams's voyage, aside from the crew, 372 passengers set out:

---

[13] Newspaper report: Sacramento Union, Sep 7th 1909.
[14] www.shipsnostalgia.com

	Married		Single		Children		Infants		
	Male	Female	Male	Female	Male	Female	Male	Female	Totals
Full Paying	0	0	1	2	0	0	0	0	**3**
Free	29	31	74	75	33	25	5	7	279
Assisted	16	15	22	0	10	12	4	2	81
Other	2	1	4	2	0	0	0	0	9
Total Departed	**47**	**47**	**101**	**79**	**43**	**37**	**9**	**9**	**372**
Births							1	1	2
Deaths			1			2	2	1	6
Total Arrived	**47**	**47**	**100**	**79**	**43**	**35**	**8**	**9**	**368**
English									130
Scottish									195
Irish									43

William observed that there were 103 single men sharing the limited space, though the official figures had it at 101. In any event the space was tiny and the ceiling height of the between-deck was usually 6 to 8 feet. The beds were made of rough boards arranged along both sides. As William pointed out, the beds were a temporary arrangement since the Shenir, though converted to transport the emigrants, was designed principally to carry cargo, so clearly the passengers were accommodated in the cargo hold. The temporary furnishings could be easily removed and replaced by cargo. Once the emigrants reached their destination, the accommodation was stripped back to the requisite number of beds for any returning travellers, the boards and associated furniture typically dumped and the ship was then ready for return to Europe. To get down to the accommodation the passengers used hatch ladders. The passageway down was steep, so accidents frequently happened.

Water Quality

Typically the ship loaded up a supply of casks of drinking water sourced from Loch Katrine (which since circa 1859 had provided most of the water for Glasgow) adequate for the voyage ahead. However, emigrant, troop and other passenger vessels fitted with an efficient apparatus for distilling fresh water from salt water were permitted to sail with only half the normally required amount of water. Although there were several such machines available at the time, it is most likely that the Chaplin's Patent Distilling Apparatus with Steam pump (an early design of the device for producing fresh water on board ship) was the machine referred to here. Chaplin's manufacturing and engineering plant facilities were located at Cranstonhill Engine Works, Glasgow.

Monday 25th Sept.

We have made no progress today. Tonight the young men have collected all the musical instruments and are marching round the deck making an awful noise. When they got tired they had a dance but the dancing was a failure as there was no young woman. But they were not to be beat as they marched in procession to the Doctor and demanded the company of the girls but it was of no use. However the Doctor consented to let them down now and again. After that there was more peace. The voyage is becoming dreary as we have made no progress for two days. Today we sighted land about 4 p.m. and later on we found that the tide had carried us back to Ireland so that after 4 days sailing we may say we are still in sight of home.

Tuesday 26th Sept.

This is a beautiful morning and the ship is doing some fine sailing now we have at last got a fair wind and are on the direct road to Queensland. The number of our passengers was increased today by the addition of a little girl[15] , mother and daughter doing well. Numbers of whales and porpoises run now daily.

Weds 27th Sept

The sea is very rough today, some of the waves a good deal higher than the side of the ship, and every now and then the ship sent her bow right through them and they came sweeping along the deck as if they wanted everything with them. We had to give up all attempts to get our faces washed as it was impossible to stand without the use of both hands. We have had a splendid run in the last 24 hours at an average of 12 knots. If we keep this up we will get into warm weather in a very short time. We got our supply of flour, suet and raisins today. Our mess is all

---

[15] Baby born was E.S.Barron, daughter of Ellen and George

right as we have got a baker in it and he is quite willing to bake it. There were some strange duffs today some of them had to go to the pigs. There are three pigs on board, they seem to be doing well, it was a curious sight when they were sick. There are also six sheep and hens and ducks on board. Today we have had a good days sailing from midday yesterday till the same time today we have covered 215 miles and since then she has been sailing at an average 12 knots an hour. Such a speed is bound to produce dirty weather. When on deck you don't know the minute when a big wave may come on board and lay you flat on the deck as well as drench you to the skin if you have not been smart enough to lay hold of a rope. But even then if the rope is a slack one you may find yourself swinging round the mast as if you were doing some gymnastic exercise. All of this is of course new to me but I feel quite contented and would not turn back for a good deal. A great many would leave all their belongings to be once more on dry land. Since we lost sight of land it looks to me like we never move out of the spot. Looking round there is nothing but sea and sky. We are as it were sitting in the centre of a large pond and making no progress.

Thursday 28th Sept.

Rain fell all day. Early this morning we passed a sailing ship homeward bound and after breakfast we sighted another one going home. In the afternoon she had passed us and was out of sight. Both the vessels were too far away to be spoken to, they were

This, his first burial at sea, was surely a significant
moment for William. He would have attended
funerals at home, and would have understood the
normal burial practices and traditions. But at sea
there could be none of that - no wake, no
opportunity for family and friends beyond those on
board to pay their respects, no whiskey or feasting,

---

[16] 28th September The child who died was 7 year old Rosina Anderson, daughter of
James & Rosina.

no coffin and no family to carry it, no procession to the graveyard, and little time for the family to go through the traditional grieving process, and then no grave to visit afterwards.

Diphtheria would have been well known to most adults in 1882. It was only 4 years earlier that Queen Victoria's daughter Princess Alice had contracted the disease and two of the Queens grandchildren had died of it. Although the bacteria had been discovered in 1882 by Edwin Klebs, the first cure of a person with diphtheria was not reported until 1891 in Berlin, and it was not until 1895 that the production and testing of diphtheria antitoxin started in the United States.

Friday, Sept 29th

Fine morning and we are sailing rapidly away again. The sea is alive with whales and porpoises[17]. The whales are spouting away some of them sending water up in the air the height of about 15 feet or so. And the porpoises are the most amusing fish I ever saw. We can see them coming swimming along 4 or 5 abreast like a regiment but if one trys to go before another then comes a race. They don't seem to let another pass them until they are beat. They keep to the surface of the water so that we can always see

---

[17] Living in the 21st century when you could spend entire days out at sea without ever seeing a fish, it seems hard to believe Williams observations, but the most recent estimate is that from the introduction of commercial whaling almost 3 million whales were killed in the 20th century. *Marine Fisheries Review* (R. C. Rocha Jr, P. J. Clapham and Y. V. Ivashchenko *Mar. Fish. Rev.* **76**, 37–48; 2014)

their movement. After perhaps half a dozen of them have had a race they will turn about and start back again as even and as smart as if it was the same number of men trying a foot race. We have got a fright today with the news that measles had broken out and it has put a damper on our spirits but I don't think it will spread. The first thing we did this morning was to take up our beds and walk upstairs to the deck and give them the air which will do them good. The wind has risen to a great height, we have taken down most of the sails and are driving along with nearly bare poles at a fearful rate. Every minute it is getting worse. We got warning for this as all afternoon we were followed by a flock of Mother Careys Chickens[18] and wild duck and they quacked and squealed all the time they followed us. The sailors put great faith in these birds. When we saw them first they shook their heads and talked of lots of wind but as the flock of birds increased they commenced to curse them and wish them thousands of miles away. We passed a large steamer homeward bound in the afternoon but she was too far away to be spoken to.

Hot on the heels of the child's death, an outbreak of measles would certainly have given rise to real fear. Death from measles was extremely common at the time, and in the confined space aboard ship it would

---

[18] **Mother Careys Chickens**, or Storm Petrel, were seen as harbingers of bad weather largely because, as birds that nest on land only when breeding, during storms they took shelter in the lee of sailing ships.

have been frightening, especially for the majority of the 44 families with children. The precautions taken by the passengers on this occasion can still be seen reflected in 21st century expert advice where such illnesses remain common, such as the seasonal warnings in which it is recommended that to protect against measles, people should make sure their rooms are well ventilated, keeping the indoor air fresh, while airing bedding regularly.

Saturday 30th Sept.

Still driving before the storm at a fearful rate. I don't know what is our exact speed but I didn't think it possible for any ship to go so quick. There were some got a proper drenching today, it was something awful, the waves were coming over the side in solid water. The waves were running as high as the yard arm. Sometimes we thought we were going to be swallowed up as on either side there was nothing but walls of water about 30 feet high standing above the sides of the ship. The Captain has been under the necessity of removing the man on the lookout from the top of the forecastle to the cradle of the mast, as we might have been run down at any minute as standing where he was he could not see over the top of the waves. This is a night I don't know a word to describe it. I have just heard that all this speed is for nothing, as we are 9 points off our course. Half an hour ago we made another tack and I think we have since taken the right road. When down below you have everyone singing all sorts of songs and if you ask them to go to bed they will tell you it is Saturday night. One thing certain that with all the noise there is none of it caused by drink, rather the opposite, all the young men and sailors are wearing blue ribbons and medals given them by the Salvation Army Officers, but I expect most of them will be forfeited when we reach land as some of them have nothing to grumble at but that they had brought some spirits with them, the Emigrant Officer having made no inspection of our boxes. This the end of our first week at sea and made very little progress.

Saturday 1st October

Could not sleep last night with the rolling and pitching of the vessel. Once or twice I was nearly asleep when in an instant I was rolling backward and forward against the side of my bunk. About one o'clock in the morning we were all awakened by hearing the first mate shouting down the hatch for a Constable, these gentlemen like them at home weren't at hand when wanted. After about ten minutes one of them turned up, the mate sent him aft to watch the main hatch as he feared someone was broaching on the stores. Stationing a man at each hatch he went aft some way to fetch a revolver, then going down the forehatch he proceeded to search for the thieves. While he was going down the forehatch they were making their way out at the main hatch further aft. The Constable who was stationed there, an Irishman, he saw them coming up but instead of detaining them he looked stupefied and asked them if they saw anybody down at the stores. Of course you will have an idea of the answer they would give. Whether the Mate had no faith in this Irishman or whether he saw them coming out we don't know, at any rate he was on deck in a minute and handcuffed the two men. We had only been two days at sea when the Captain stopped the supply of butter to the sailors, this caused a great deal of grumbling and they show their discontent every time they find a chance. A few days ago they went to the chief mate and stated their grievances but he told them he could not go against the Captain. The Chief mate is well liked by everybody on board. Since then things have got worse and we found the men refusing to work, but this morning this was the means those two took of showing their discontent. On making an inspection below we found that they had not been down below for provisions but had opened some of the passengers chests and looked out some good clothes for themselves. How long they will be kept in irons I do not know but today we can see them get their biscuit and water handed into them. This crime I believe is one the Captain can't deal with so he will likely release them, and arrest them on sighting Australia. We had no service today owing to the storm.

Monday 2nd October.

Could not sleep last night at all. Just fancy when you go to bed the vessel may be riding over the waves from {stem to stern} that would send us to sleep. But just as you are losing your senses she commences to rock from side to side that keeps us awake and so on. During the night you can never fix yourself on one position for as soon as you are fixed you get a heave and you have got to do it over again. Went up on deck before breakfast and had a wash in salt water. The marine soap won't raise a lather, it is like rubbing your face with the soft side of a brick. After breakfast we went on deck to enjoy the brilliant sun which is yet not too hot for us although some day soon it will scorch us. We sighted two sailing vessels and one steamer today and they are all going to Australia although we are all steering in a different direction. Before night however we got ahead and lost sight of the whole lot. This helped to raise our spirits as it gave us an idea of what our vessel actually could do when put to it. I forgot to mention that the library was opened last week, it contains above 150 books. It is kept by the Salvation Army Captain who is also schoolmaster on board {it is on the deck}. The library is down in the married quarters in the centre of the ship. It was a beautiful night before we went to bed. The sky was perfectly clear and the number of falling stars was considerable.

"Falling Stars"

The display of shooting stars could have been the Orionids meteor shower, active each year between 2nd October and the 7th November. These are the remnants left behind by Haley's comet, not due again until 2061. Alternatively, and as reported by astronomers around that time, the meteor shower could have been the Camelopardalids, a minor shower emanating from a comet. These brief streaks of light were expected to peak on 3rd October 1882.

However, given the proximity of the then famous Great September Comet, which William saw at 4 a.m. the following morning, it is surely more likely that the meteor shower was associated with that comet.

William again refers to the comet on the morning of 6th October, when he also referred to a rather strange and unexplained sighting of "two moons". This effect was in fact the result of the comet splitting into several pieces on 30th September, and was officially recorded as such by the Chief Assistant of the Royal Observatory at Cape Town, W.H.Finlay, who had been the first to record observations of the comet on 7th September. The comet remained visible to the naked eye into February of 1883. Its tail was estimated to be 4 to 6 degrees long until the middle of February. Williams reference to it as "the comet", rather than "a comet" suggests he had been aware of it prior to setting out on his voyage. There are not many first hand non-astronomer accounts of the comet extant, although the following article which appeared in the **Hawkes Bay Herald** on 21st September 1882 demonstrates what a sensation the comet was, and poking fun at many of those claiming to have seen it:

An Honest Reporter – *This is what the reporter of the Hawkes Bay Herald saw of the comet:-"Yesterday small knots of citizens could be seen at every shady corner, peeping round as if they were dodging bailiffs or mothers-in-law. Inquiry elicited the information that they were looking for the comet. We were foolish enough to get a "crick in the neck" by looking upward, to experience temporary blindness by trying to stare the sun out of countenance (a task which proved too much even for a reporters "cheek") and to run the risk of making that blindness permanent by "speering" through bits of broken beer bottles. The result was – nothing. Others avowed that they saw the comet, and entered into elaborate descriptions of its appearance, even to stating the shape, size, and colour of its tail. We did not say what we thought about these asseverations because we like peace, and dislike black eyes.*

Tuesday 3rd Oct.

Got wakened by one of the sailors at 4 a.m. to rise and see the comet and it was a sight worth seeing. I wouldn't have missed it for a good deal. We could see it plainly travelling across the sky with a shower of sparks or stars about 4 or 5 yards long. As we are now close on the equator we are at the spots for seeing some beautiful sights in the heavens and it is so close and warm. I will have to try and find a sleeping place on deck where it will be cooler. We took our beds up on deck today to get the fresh air for it was so close last night that this morning our bunks have a horrid smell. The beds have to go up on deck every Tuesday and Saturday and the place washed out these days, and scraped and swept. The other mornings the messes take time about at cleaning. Today it is warmer and the heat will increase every day until we pass the Line. In the afternoon we sighted a large steamer homeward bound. Scarcely a day has passed since we have left but we have seen vessels going one way or another. This afternoon the two sailors who were locked up were liberated and are again at their work, but one of them only is to be handed over to the Queensland government. He deserves it too if all stories be true. The sailors say that he is just done with six months in Duke Street, he has often been in prison. The offence he will be charged with is a very serious one. It seems that they not only cut the ropes of one of the chests but on being detected they threw down a lamp they had and the cover coming off the naked lamp was left burning. The stock of gunpowder and signal apparatus was lying not far off and if they had taken fire the ship and all it contained would have been some other where than Queensland. The ship is scudding along splendid. This day has been longer by an hour than yesterday owing to us going nearer the sun. There is hope that we will spend the New Year in Queensland yet, although our first weeks sailing was not up to much. We sighted a sailing vessel just before dark.

Duke Street

A Glasgow Song

There is a happy land, doon Duke Street Jail,

Where a' the prisoners stand, tied tae a nail.

Ham an' eggs they never see, dirty watter fur yer tea;

there they live in misery, God Save the Queen!

Wednesday 4th October.

Today we are sailing first class. The Captain has ordered up extra sails. Those extra ones are put up on long poles or yards. The yards are put out first at the end of the fore main yard and then the sails are run up, one on the underside and the other on the topside. They call them stansails and when all the sail is up it is a great cloud of canvas. We expect to reach the trade winds in about 24 hours if this speed keeps up. We had a meeting tonight held by the Salvationists. After this meeting was over some of us went into the forecastle and spent the evening with the sailors where we had a nights singing. These men rough as they are they care for no songs better than they do for those of home. One song sung by one of them sent my thoughts back to Peebles. The name of it was "Theres a Smile for me at Home"[19], and I could not help wishing there was some means or other of letting my friends know how I was and of learning how all my friends and companions were keeping but it was no use sighing as I must wait and hope for the best. Today we are attracted by seeing a small bird flying about the rigging of the ship seemingly quite at home as it came and landed sometimes where we might have caught it. It was like a bullfinch and some of the chaps said they had seen it every day since we left. It will come to no harm from us however as it takes our thoughts back to Scotland. It is a fine clear night.

---

[19] A copy of this ballad is at Kent State University, reference "Street Ballads of Victorian England, Cara Gilgenbach, May 13, 2002", Box 2, Folder 166

There's a Smile Waiting for Me at Home

Written by the Late Harry Clifton

Troubles we fancy are heavy to bear,

In trav'ling lifes's dreary way,

Some are heartbroken with sorrow and care,

Others are cheerful and gay.

The road may be rough and the journey be long

As over its pathway I roam,

Contented I sing, this the theme of my song,

There's a smile waiting for me at home.

Chorus:

The frowns of the world they're nothing to me

Trials and troubles may come,

I've this consolation, where'er I may be,

There's a smile waiting for me at home.

Weary and worn, and by labour opress'd,

Or sneer'd at by fools in their pride,

The shrine of my love and the heaven of rest,

I find at my own fireside.

Voices so gentle and hearts that are warm,

To cheer me when sorrow should come,

I know I've a shelter from ev'ry storm,

In the smiles that await me at home[20].

---

[20] From a copy in my own collection

Thursday 5th October

It was very hot today. We expected to get into the chests before this to get our light clothes but we have never seen them yet. The ship itself has got on lighter clothing as all the sails that were up when we left Glasgow have been taken down and lighter ones put up. The reason for this is that for the next 6 weeks or so we will have nothing but light winds and the Mate says they will be strong enough. But it is not right as the sails just taken down were those inspected by the Board of Trade and pronounced by them to be fit to carry us to Queensland. The sailors say that if they had seen the thin rags that have been hung up today they never would have passed them. We have been complaining daily to the Doctor about the cooking and yesterday he told the cook if it was not better next time he would give him the sack. Seemingly he has paid attention to this as we could not wish for better. After dinner we went and complimented him on his success but he thought we were taking our fun of him as he swore an awful oath that if he met any of us in Queensland he would swing for us. About teatime we sighted a schooner some distance away and on getting a look at her through a glass we can see her topmasts are gone with the effects of the late gale. After tea we see another sailing ship and she seems to be a pretty large one. She is standing away between us and the sun. It has much the same effect as a cloud would have because the sun is lying so low she almost covers it up as she passes.

Friday 6th October.

I was up on deck soon in the morning. Two hours in the cool is worth the whole day. Just before breakfast we sighted the coast of Madeira but we could not see it very plain. It was just like a cloud. Before many hours we had passed it and it was out of sight. The heat today is something dreadful and although we lie down in the shade the sweat pours from us. Early this morning just as the comet appeared we saw two moons in the sky or perhaps the second was the reflection of the first. Today there are some programs of a concert to be held tomorrow night posted up in a few prominent places about the ship. What the concert will be like we cant tell yet but the names in the programme include some good singers both among passengers and sailors.

Madeira as William may have seen it, by John Glover (1767-1849)[21]

---

[21] The original work is held at The National Gallery of Australia

Saturday 7th October

Today we are in a sea as smooth as glass, not a ripple on the surface, there being no wind and the heat is 96 in the shade. Our faces and hands are already as brown as nuts, some are losing their skin the heat is so strong. After dinner we sighted a large ship in front of us and coming up behind us we can just see the topsails of another. At 6 p.m. the concert began. We go aft to the poop where the girls are and get a seat wherever we can. Some are on deck, some are in the boats and others are stuck up among the rigging and the girls are upon the poop. One of the married men was appointed Chairman and he opened the concert with rather a long speech. When done the first song was sung by one of the sailors, then followed one by a married woman who has a splendid voice. I am certain she has sung in public before as there was no fear or nervousness about her. One of the songs she sang was entitled "Write me a Letter from Home", a very pretty song when sung with effect. The chorus is

"Oh have they forgot me at home/ Or do they expect me to come

Oh go and tell them from me/ To write me a letter from home"[22]

Two of the young men sang next, then followed the cook with a medley which took very well but was a lot of nonsense, and some others gave some short

---

[22] Words & Music by Will. S. Hays (See Library of Congress, Rare Book and Special Collections Division, *America Singing: Nineteenth-Century Song Sheets*)

pieces. Altogether the concert was a success but there was none of the single girls to give us a song. During the concert the wind rose and all the sails were trimmed, and by the time the singers were done we were sailing at the rate of 12 knots and the prospect of going still faster by morning.

Sunday 8th October

It was cooler down below last night as there was such a wind blowing, it was cooler than it has been for some time. The mate says we had 6 hours rougher weather last night than we have had since we started. It is not much better this morning as she is shipping water at almost every plunge. The heat is so strong that you are no sooner wet than you are dry again so we pay little attention to the sea now. But today we keep a weather eye open as there is to be a muster at 10 a.m. when we are to appear in our best clothes. This muster did not take place , the Doctor being one of the most timid men on board. Whenever we see the waves coming higher than the side of the ship you never see the Doctor. This is one of the days when you walk the deck you have to stretch your legs on each side of you to keep you up. If you want to cross the deck you have only to wait till she gives a lurch to that side and you are slid down to your destination, if not on your feet on something else which makes you feel uncomfortable. About midday we sighted a large sailing vessel a little in front of us. Before many hours we have passed her and when signalled she turns out to be a ship that left Glasgow about 10 days before us with Emigrants bound for New Zealand. We bid it farewell by lowering the flag 3 times. The signalling is all done with flags. When we get wind we can sail , the sailors themselves say she can get up a speed they seldom see but we have been unlucky in getting good winds. At night we had a religious service held by the Salvationists, the Doctor not having turned out all day. After church the wind changed and all hands were called out to put the ship about. The sailors while pulling the ropes of the main sail or any heavy pull always sing a chorus and the one they were at today was "Bring whisky for me Johnie" while a few moments before they were joining in the chorus of the hymns. It is mere habit and they always do it when at the capstan or ropes.

Whiskey-o, Johnny-o

John rise her up from down below

Whiskey, whiskey, whiskey-o

Up aloft this yard must go

John rise her up from down below

8th October

It is fascinating to observe Williams changing attitude towards the ship's Doctor during the journey. From his initial respect during the solemn burial ceremony, later on seeing him as a bit of a coward when the Doctor stays below during the rough weather; then focussing in on his German nationality, his poor use of the English language and his unsatisfactory communication skills. Ultimately William develops a strong ill-feeling towards the Doctor for his neglect of the one single man who died on board, culminating in the signing of a complaint against him.

The ship sighted on 8th October was the Nelson, under Captain Bannatyne, out of Greenock and heading for Port Chalmers, where they arrived on 25th December 1882. They were carrying 59 passengers. She was a passenger & cargo vessel, built in 1874 by Robert Duncan for Patrick Henderson. Dimensions 239' x 36' x 21':

The Nelson at Wellington, NZ [23]

The Nelson sailed from 1874 to 1902.

[23] *White Wings Vol. 1: Fifty years of sail in the New Zealand trade, 1850 to 1900,* The New Zealand Electronic Text Collection, http://nzetc.victoria.ac.nz/tm/scholarly/tei-Bre01Whit-t1-body-d43-d1.html#Bre01Whit-fig-Bre01Whit104a.gif, covered by the Creative Commons Share-Alike license

Monday 9th October

This morning there was a great storm of thunder and lightning and the rain pouring down upon us at a fearful rate. After dinner the rain cleared off, and some of them had a game of quoits. The quoits were made of rope which the sailors spliced together. The distance was marked off with a piece of chalk, and two sides chosen, the married against the single men, the latter being victorious. Just before teatime we had a pretty stiff breeze which sent the vessel flying along at a great speed. You have no idea how it raises our spirits when she is flying through the water. The rain fell heavily all the rest of the night making us turn into bed early, there to read for an hour or two till we fell asleep.

Thursday 10th October

This morning we are still flying ahead and we managed to keep up the speed the whole day. At 6 a.m. we got our chests sent up on deck. There is scarcely room for so many on deck and as everyone wants a little extra room to lay something down while he takes out it is a great scramble. It is like some great sale as there is nothing on deck but people running backward and forward with bundles of old and new clothes in their arms. The appearance of the passengers in the afternoon is neat and clean as the most of them are in their whites and all sorts of hats. I have got on my whites and my big white hat. We look fine going about the deck. The women are busy washing the dirty clothes of their husbands and children. Even with the small number of married couples on board one can see every phase of domestic life. In the majority of cases the women are the masters, they seem to think this is a pleasure trip for them, while the men have to empty all the pots and do all the dirty work. One woman who was washing today got angry at a little child that was hanging on to her skirts and after giving the child a knock that sent it down on deck, she left it there and marched away down the hatchway saying she would let her husband see he didn't come here to play. Whatever she said I don't know but in a few minutes she appeared on deck with a triumphant look, while the husband was looking as if someone had stolen his scone. Some hours later I saw the same man sitting with the child as if he were there under a penalty. Another case of a little boy about 10 years of age, he was sent down stairs by his mother to go and tell his father he was a liar. She was doing nothing but sitting on deck in the heat of the sun when her infant came to her crying. She sent the boy down for his father to take care of the child, he sent back word that he was busy and the boy was sent down again with that message, with the result that the father came up at once and took the child while the woman enjoyed herself.

Wednesday 11th October

This morning the first thing we saw when we went on deck was the largest of the Canary Islands "Tenerife", 12236 feet high. It was like a cloud, but before breakfast it was plainer and we could then see for ourselves that it was land. The breeze has again died down and we are lying rolling like a log in the water under the heat of a burning sun. Truly when there is no wind the heat is something terrific. After breakfast we saw a pilot fish sailing about a foot just in front of the bow of the vessel, and was there the whole day. This is a very pretty fish, it is about the size of a mackerel and striped the same way, only the stripes are deep red over the back, when seen sparkling in the sun it is very pretty. We tried almost all forenoon to catch it but met with no success, it refusing all sorts of bait so we let it have its own way. We were told that this fish is seldom seen but that there is a shark not far off. We not being allowed at the stern of the vessel we could not see if it was the case this time. The shark will feed on almost any kind of fish but this one, whatever is the reason. The sailors say the shark has no scent and the pilot fish has a double allowance therefore it is able to trace out food for the larger one. About noon today the heat had almost skinned us. After teatime we sighted 4 vessels all homeward bound and I hear a rumour that there is a chance of getting a letter home if you should meet any steamers. Now we are in fine weather it will be quite easy for a vessel to come alongside. The passengers today are thankful they have their light clothing, especially in the afternoon. When there is a breath of wind it is so cool to feel it blowing around you. One of the Highland men has got out his kilt and pipes, and marching the deck blowing away. He had to give it up after a short time however as he couldn't keep his feet with the rolling of the vessel. Sometimes the ship gave a lurch and sent him flying against the sides when the bagpipes would give a squeal and spoil the tune. The pipes were voted a failure. He said he could play if he could march and to march was almost impossible. I wasn't sorry when they were given up as I don't think the player was one of the best. Some of the young men after it was dark went along to the poop and made an attempt to speak to the girls but they got a cooler. The Captain had noticed them and got a bucket of water and just as they were having a good laugh at something that had been said, he sent the water among them sending them off in double quick time, the girls being ordered below at once.

Thursday 12th October

We saw this morning another of the Canary Islands, a much smaller one than the first one we saw. One of the ships we saw last night we have passed and we are rapidly gaining on one right ahead. After breakfast we came up almost within half a mile of her and as we were passing the Captain spoke to her. She had been 4 weeks from Newcastle and was bound for the Chilean coast with a cargo of coals. This was the first vessel I had seen being spoken to and it was a very interesting sight. We were the first to speak, our captain running up 4 different flags which hung until the other vessel sent up 4 flags of different colours in answer. Ours were then taken down and some others run up and so on for about half an hour. At the end of the conversation each ship ran up the English ensign and dipped it 3 times as a farewell. We were going so much faster than this vessel that although she was carrying the same sail as we were yet we lost sight of her within a couple of hours.

Friday 13th October

A splendid morning and a glorious sunrise. The sun rises here as quick as it sets. There is no twilight, there may be broad daylight and 10 minutes after it is dark. In the morning it is just the same, daylight coming in like a crack. At 6 a.m. one of the sheep was killed. Shortly after breakfast we saw a couple of flying fish but they were a long distance away. Now we are into the trade winds we are making fair progress. Today we have been all alone on the water, no vessels being in sight. Just at sunset we can see the topsails of a vessel but cant tell yet which way she is going. The first sight we get of a vessel you would think she was sunk, only seeing her topmasts. Of all the ships we have passed we haven't seen the hull of half a dozen of them. As the sun disappears so does the wind, we being almost at a standstill but before morning it is hard to say how stiff we may get it.

Saturday 14th October

Flying along at a pretty pace this morning, something like 13 knots an hour. I hope we will get this wind all through the tropics. There is a large vessel in sight going the same way we are. After breakfast we saw a great many flying fish, these fish are increasing in number everyday as we get into warmer weather, they can fly a good deal further than I imagined. Sometimes they fly the whole length of the ship and I have seen them fly a good deal further. The sailors this afternoon played a trick on the girls on the poop. When we got our chests a few days ago a good many of the passengers gave their cast off clothing to the sailors. It was with some of these old clothes they had made up in the form of a man which they stuffed with hay, then strapped it on a cross made with boards and then lowered it into the water. We were not going very fast at the time and as the dummy floated past the stern a number of the girls set up a scream, but in a few minutes they saw what it was and as we saw it disappearing in the distance we wished him a prosperous voyage. At 6 p.m. we had another concert, this time there was no female singers and it was scarcely so good as the last one. Still always something turns up. To get a view of the singers and to hear properly, some of the young chaps crawled into the rigging and some of the boats. The Captain evidently meant mischief, as before the concert began he had the pump brought aft and the second mate stood at the head of the poop stair with the nozzle in his hand ready to let fly at a moment's notice. On went the concert flourishing and as it got darker, on to the boats went the single men. About an hour after the start the boats were full, and by this time it was pitch dark.

The Captain gave the word and the pump was set a going and these young men came dripping one after another on deck with a splash, drenched to the skin while the captain ordered the sailors to pump away apparently quite regardless how they got out, so long as he got them out at all.

Sunday 15th October

We are still keeping up our pace and this is delightful as there are hopes of us getting landed before the New Year yet. This is a splendid day and the first good Sunday we have had. The Doctor called a muster at 10 a.m., every man appearing clean and tidy. After muster we attended church and listened to the Doctor reading one of Spurgeons[24] sermons after which he read a short prayer out of an English prayer book, and then the Salvationists Captain gave a short address and then the service closed. The girls came down on deck to the service, that is the only time we get near them and even then there is a rope between us. There are a good many Roman Catholics on board. They went below and held a service among themselves. I went down to hear them before they were finished and every man of them was on his knees repeating prayers and crossing themselves all the time. It had the appearance this morning of being

---

[24] *Charles Spurgeon, a Baptist preacher, was the pastor of the congregation of the New Park Street Chapel in London for 38 years. He also founded Spurgeon's College. An author, he is most famous for his sermons.*

*a very warm day and as the day advances the heat is
getting greater. Expecting this we have on as few
clothes as we can decently carry. In the afternoon a
bible class was begun on the forecastle head and
attended by a number of the young men on board.
The opening text was from the 15th chapter of Johns
gospel which we read. The Second Steward (a young
man who is going on this voyage to make some
money to finish his time at college when he intends
to visit foreign countries as a missionary) then took
up the subject and spoke for half an hour. He is a
splendid speaker and could lay it off beautiful. I
enjoyed it far better than the service in the forenoon.
At the close of the class we were told that any of us
who had friends on the poop could get aft to speak to
them for an hour. It is a curious fact that mostly all
the young men suddenly remembered that their
cousin or sister was on the poop. I don't think they
will be allowed back again they having abused the
privilege by making too much noise. After tea we had
an evening service held by the Salvationists but it was
surprising how few attended the meeting. Nobody
seemed to take any interest in their preaching it
being too much of the Publican and Pharisee style. It
brought me in mind of the Plymouth Brethren[25] at
home.*

---

[25] Plymouth Brethren

Originating from Anglicanism, the Plymouth Brethren are a conservative, non-conformist Christian movement whose history is said to be traced to Dublin in the 1820s.

(For an account, see: Abigail, Shawn (June 2006). "What is the history of the 'Brethren'?")

Monday 16th October

Scarcely slept a wink last night with the heat. When we went on deck this morning there seemed to be a new rule made through the night, as we were not allowed to pass a certain line on deck. It was from some of them making a noise last night and so we have no part of the ship but the fore part and the majority of the work goes on there. To keep within this line we were continually in somebodys way. We miss the liberty very much as there was a fine seat on either side of the ship with two spare spars. We had the liberty of going on to the married peoples part of the deck, so we had a good deal of room. One English chap went past the bounds but the first mate took him by the cuff of the neck and put him back again. This was a lesson to the rest and it wasn't attempted afterwards. Today we had our first supply of lime juice given us, and it is a preferable drink to the warm water we have been drinking for some time. In the afternoon we sighted a sailing vessel going ahead of us. This same vessel was in sight yesterday and we are still the same distance off her, but we have hopes of catching her before many hours. About tea we had something new to amuse us in the shape of a fight. Two women had for some time disagreed, and this afternoon when they met on deck they revived their quarrel with the result that one of them raised her fist and let fly at the other ones face. The blow was returned and it looked as though it was going to be a regular stand up affair when a Constable came upon the scene and took them both to the Doctor who listened to them and the account of the fight and dismissed them with an admonition. When they were coming back some of the young men cheered them as they passed. After it was dark the young men assembled at the line that had been drawn this morning and with their musical instruments set up the most discordant din I ever heard, it was for nothing else but mischief.

Tuesday 17th October

A deputation of young men waited on the Doctor and made a protest regarding our food with the result that we have got an increased supply of water and some other things are to be increased and properly cooked so we hope to be better fed in the future, we are not bad off on the whole. The deputation also asked for greater space on deck and this was granted, we are now allowed to go on to the married quarters again. The vessel we saw last night we are gradually passing too, having caught up on her during the night and we are now fast leaving her astern. Today I hear there are three girls on biscuit and water, two of them for lifting a piece of bread and the other for lifting some currents that didn't belong to them, they have each got 3 days. I see sitting before me a large bird, it is either a crane or a heron. It has been flying about almost all day and we did our best to keep it from resting on the ship till after dark, and then when it is asleep we mean to try and catch it. The attempt has been made once or twice since dark but we are in too big a hurry as the bird hasn't had time to fall asleep.

Wednesday 18th October

I slept all night on deck it is so very hot below, it was very pleasant sleeping on deck as it was so cool. About 2 a.m. our winged visitor from the coast of Africa was caught by one of the sailors. The attempt to escape was terrific as with its beak it made various attempts to bite him. Its bill is about 5 inches long as it tapers to the point as sharp as a needle. There was such a noise over the catching of this bird that the Captain came forward to see what the row was about. He threatened to put us all below if we didn't behave as the sailors must have their sleep. We were all wakened that were sleeping on deck and helped to make more noise. They tied it to the mast and it has been stalking about all morning. About 10 o clock the Doctor came along and looked at it and offered the sailor a pound of tobacco for it which was accepted at once with the question if he would give that for every bird that they would catch. In the afternoon I heard that the bird had been killed and was being stuffed. We saw the enemy of the Flying Fish today, the Dolphin. There were hundreds of fish to be seen today. Behind the dolphins came a shoal of Bonitoes[26], followed by as many bottle-nosed

---

[26] Bonitos are swift, predacious fishes found worldwide. They have striped backs and silvery bellies and grow to a length of about 30 inches. Like tuna, they are streamlined, with a forked tail, and a row of small finlets. Other fish sometimes called "bonito" include skipjack tuna.

whales, and later on we had our weather guides, the Porpoises. When they appear the wind is sure to increase and the more fish there is the more wind we get. People who have never been on the ocean would not believe how many fish there are in the sea. I never imagined there was as many.

Thursday 19th October

We had to take our beds upon deck and also our bed boards to give them a proper wash to keep down disease. We will do all in our power to prevent it, at the same time it doesn't all lie with us. Out of the hold there was brought up about a dozen bags of potatoes all in a most rotten state and the smell was sickening. They were all thrown overboard. This is the way the best of the meat goes, half a boatload of turnips and cabbages having met the same fate a day or two ago. Now these turnips would have been a treat to us if we had got a share of them when they were going but as they were reserved for the cabin and they couldn't eat the supply, they got leave to waste. Today we saw the first appearance of the shark, a number of them following the ship for some time. Some Bonitoes followed us the most of the day and after sunset the sailors tried to catch some for breakfast. Two of these went out on the jib boon and a hook and a piece of rag on it for a bait to imitate the flying fish, they succeeded in catching half a dozen. One of them weighed 9 lb, their take in all was about 40 lb. We sighted a steamer homeward bound but it was a long way off. Later we sighted another one but our Captain is too anxious to make a quick passage to stop to let us send letters home, but we signalled to it so you will most likely see us spoken to in the papers. After dark we got a sample of tropical showers, it was an awful shower, the lightning was flashing across the sky.

Fresh fowl and fish was a welcome change from "preserved meat" for any sailors or passengers that could catch them on these voyages. Of course the ones who would have benefited most were those passengers in steerage, particularly nursing mothers and children. William clearly felt very strongly about the appalling waste of good food thrown overboard, which could have been used earlier in the voyage to improve the nourishment value of their diet. For state aided emigrants there had been since 1850 a proscribed minimum provisions allowance that included:

Daily - 3 quarts water; Weekly - 2 ½ lbs bread or biscuit; 2 lbs rice; 1 lb wheatflour; 3 lbs oatmeal; ½ lb sugar; ½ lb molasses; 2 oz tea.

Children under 14 were allowed just half of the adult allowance.

Although every ship was different, it seems that the food provided to the poorest passengers was often a significant improvement on the diet they were used to at home, and some reports from the time suggest that, despite the hardships, many emigrants thrived while on the journey.

Friday 20th October

A splendid morning. We sighted a large ship ahead of us but couldn't tell which way it was going, and we passed one in the morning. We got something new today, we actually got some jam. What we got this for I do not know unless it was a substitute for onions, of the latter we got none with our fresh meat today. I don't care though if we never get them again. We had each about half a pound of jam when it was divided. Almost the whole day some of the young men have been trying the fishing but without success. We have met up on the ship we saw in the morning and signalled her. She is the Inch Murren from Glasgow for Sydney with a general cargo and a few passengers 23 days out, "6 days after us". It is a sight. At nights now there is a lot of wildfire flying about.

INCH MURREN OF GLASGOW, PETRIE, MASTER, BURTHEN 1254 TONS

FROM THE PORT OF GLASGOW TO SYDNEY, NEW SOUTH WALES, 23RD DECEMBER 1882

Surname	Given name	Station	Age	Of what Nation	Status	Comments
PETRIE	J N	MASTER			CREW	
MCDINALD	D	MATE	33	STORNOWAY	CREW	
DEANS	HARRY	2ND MATE	24	AYR	CREW	
HAMILTON	ALEXR	CARPENTER	39	LAMLASH	CREW	
CUNNINGHAM	Wm	STEWARD	32	GREENOCK	CREW	
MACKIE	JOHN	COOK	35	ABERDEEN	CREW	
PURDON	THOMAS	SAILS	25	GLASGOW	CREW	
TOILA	THOMAS	BOATSWAIN	31	GLASGOW	CREW	
PEDESSEN	AL	A. B.	22	NORWAY	CREW	
LAXEN	J	A. B.	23	NORWAY	CREW	
O'CONNELL	TIMOTHY	A. B.	25	CORK	CREW	FAILED TO JOIN
KLAUSSEN	LARS	A. B.	29	SWEDEN	CREW	
JOHNSON	CARL	A. B.	40	SWEDEN	CREW	
CASKIE	HENRY	A. B.	24	ARGYLE	CREW	
GALEY	H	A. B.	22	HAMBURG	CREW	
LOGON	H	A. B.	23	FINLAND	CREW	
NORAAS	REINHART	A. B.	22	NORWAY	CREW	
CAMERON	JAMES	A. B.	39	GLASGOW	CREW	
MCINALLY	MICHL	A. B.	19	DUMBARTON	CREW	
BYRNES	JOHN	A. B.	20	CORK	CREW	
MCAFFER	MALCOLM	A. B.	35	ISLAG	CREW	
MCPHERSON	ALLAN	A. B.	19	SKYE	CREW	
SINCLAIR	THOS	O. S.	16	GLASGOW	CREW	
MCKAY	PETER	A. B.	22	SKYE	CREW	FAILED TO JOIN
WELSH	JAMES	SAILORS MATE	30	SALTCOATS	CREW	
GLEN	RICHD B	3RD MATE	19	GLASGOW	CREW	INDENT'S EXPIRED
ANCELL	JMS SHIRLAW	APPRENTICE	16		CREW	
BOYD	ROBERT	APPRENTICE	18		CREW	
MCINTYRE	JOHN	APPRENTICE	15		CREW	
ROBERTSON	ANDREW	APPRENTICE	16		CREW	
WOOD	R P MR			PASSENGER	CABIN	

Source: State Records Authority of New South Wales

Saturday 21st October

The Inch Murren is still in sight, during the night she had crossed our bows and passed us but our Captain detected her and trimming up his sails she was left behind again. We spoke to another vessel, the Maggie Plimsoll from London for Sydney, no passengers. I hear that at 2 a.m. we had another death on board, this time an infant scarcely a year old. It fell into decline and after a night of great pain died. Before breakfast it was buried in the deep with all ceremony. There is scarcely a married woman on board without a very young child, and their children stand a very poor chance of life while the mothers get no proper nourishment. The only difference in their diet from ours is that they get a bottle of stout daily and sometimes a little beef tea. In the afternoon we had to take in all sail expecting a squall. In about half an hour it came across us blowing at a fearful rate but only for about an hour. When it passed away there was the Inch Murren again away ahead of us and nearly out of sight. Tonight we had no concert, last Saturdays water putting a damper on the officials. We had a nights amusement among ourselves singing songs and some of the sailors dancing. The night is very black and there are signs of rain.

The Maggie Plimsoll was possibly named in honour of Samuel Plimsoll, the renowned Liberal social reformer and champion of safety for mariners, who wrote the following:

Whoever you are who read this, help the poor sailors, for the love of God. If you are a man of influence, call a meeting and confer on this Appeal; if you are not, and will write to me, I will try to show you how to help.

If you refuse—but this I cannot think—but if you refuse or neglect to use your influence, before another year has run its course at least five hundred—five hundred men !—now in life, will strew the bottom of the sea with their dead, unburied, unresting bodies, and desolation and woe will have entered many and many a now happy home; but if you do render your help, we can secure such life-preserving activity in precautionary measures that the sailor will have no fear ; and then the storms of winter may come, but with good tight ships under them, and sound gear to their hands, their own strong arms and stout hearts can do the rest, and as, after a night of storm and tempest, which but for your fraternal care would have overwhelmed them in death and sent bereavement and anguish into their humble homes, they reach their desired haven, weary and worn it may be, but still safe—chilled to the marrow, but still alive—the blessings of those who are ready to perish shall be yours : nor shall there be lacking to you those richer blessings promised by the Great Father of us all, to those who visit the widow and fatherless, for that to the high and the noble and the sacred duty of visiting them in their affliction, you have preferred the higher, the nobler, and the yet more sacred duty of saving women and children from so sad a fate.

SAMUEL PLIMSOLL.

111, Victoria Street, London, S.W.
March, 1873.

Sunday 22nd October

This morning the rain came down in torrents wetting through all those who were sleeping on deck. I didn't happen to be one of the unfortunates. It doesn't take time to rain here, it pours. Perhaps you will be able to form an idea when I tell you that in an hours time all the small boats and empty barrels on deck were nearly filled. This had been prepared for as we wanted soft water for washing our clothes. Those on deck were in a sorry plight and looked like drowned rats as they came rushing down stairs with their shirts clinging to their skin. The sailors could have prevented them from getting wet but it was good fun for them to let them lie and see them scrambling out of the water. We had to muster again today and answer to our names, then the service after it. One of the sailors tolled the bell for a few minutes to call everybody aft. The Doctor seems to be no preacher and a bad reader, he is a German and his English is not very distinct. We are not sailing very well today, the breeze is very light and the sea is as smooth as glass. When out on the bow you can see down into the water for a great depth. I noticed some pretty specimens of sea anemones away down in the deep while nearer the surface there was lots of the commoner kind all sorts of colours the most of them being red, white or purple. We saw some more sharks sneaking about but they didn't wait long. Some of the largest whales we have seen made their appearance today, one of them I am sure was 25 foot long. They must have been very oily as when they disappeared from the surface they left the water quite calm and smooth with the oil off their bodies. In the afternoon we were in expectation of another fall of water, but it passed away behind us. It was a curious sight to see it travelling across the ocean while the sun was shining through the cloud. You need never be wet at sea as you get at the very least about half an hours notice before it begins to rain. Many a time since I came on board have I seen the sailors turn out in *their oilskins when I thought the day was one of the best that could be wished for. But I noticed they never were far wrong. It means to be a race between us and the Inch Murren as we are again ahead of her, later on she shows us a clean pair of heels as she is not to be seen anywhere.*

Monday 23rd October

A beautiful morning but no wind, we are becalmed and the prospect of a very hot day. After breakfast we saw two pilot fish followed by a couple of sharks. One of the sailors just come down from aloft says he can see thirteen vessels, we can see five from the deck all like ourselves doing nothing. It is so hot today the tar is melting out of the deck. I was washing some clothes today it was not such a bad job. At night we had some singing and dancing. Tonight the Captain set off a number of rockets for what reason I don't know.

Tuesday 24th October

We are still lying becalmed in the same spot as yesterday having never moved through the night. We are near the equator and the heat is as strong as it can be. The pitch is coming out the beams of the deck and you have to be careful where you sit down or you may stick. There are 14 ships in sight of the rigging and 5 of the deck. There are some sharks and porpoises swimming about. The sailors caught a young shark today, about 3 or 4 feet long. They cut it up and had it for tea. We had another very heavy shower this afternoon, it was welcome as it helped to keep down the heat. The wind has risen a little since the sunset and we are sailing along slowly but it is preferable to no sailing at all.

Wednesday 25th October

There is not much wind today and dull with showers of rain. There are eight ships in sight today. There are a lot of Mother Careys Chickens flying about. The Doctor caught three of them with a line and hook. They pick up anything that is thrown out of the ship. They are small black birds with some white about their neck. We always do a little sailing at night but the wind goes away as soon as the sun rises.

Thursday 26th October

Dull with gusts of wind and rain. There is a great many ships in sight today, I counted no less than 30, it was a fine sight, among them being all kinds of ships and all nationalities one of them being a man of war vessel. We signalled to one or two of them. In the afternoon we had a squall which drove us about 50 miles on our way before it passed over us. It was a curious sight to see the effect of the squall and how little water it covered. Between us and the point from where it came, there were 5 or 6 vessels lying abreast as the dark cloud moved on we could see the furthest off ships sailing swiftly through the water while all the others were lying quite still, but by and by it came over us one by one and when it passed away we were all lying abreast of each other the same as before. This was all the sailing we did the whole day.

Friday 27th October

What a morning, the rain is coming down in drops as large as beans and it continued the whole forenoon. In the afternoon it cleared away and was a splendid day afterwards. There were 16 vessels lying beside us today. We got a light breeze during the night that took us away from those that were heavy laden. There was one of the young men caught in the act of sending a letter to one of the girls on the poop. He was taken before the doctor and got put on biscuit and water for six days. This sentence is nothing but a mere form, the provisions for the culprit is kept off his mess. Instead of getting meat for 10 they only get for nine, while they get the extra biscuit. But his mess mates divide equal what is brought down so it is not much of a punishment. For the second offence he is to be put in irons. The girl the letter was sent to got the same punishment.

Saturday 28th October

We have sailed steadily the whole night and in the morning we are still doing a little. For 10 days[27] I do not think we have sailed a mile while the sun was shining unless when there was a squall and they

---

[27] In the Doldrums, within 5 degrees north and south of the Equator, it was typical for sailing ships to be becalmed, often for as long as 2 weeks.

don't last very long. Our sailing has been all through the night lately but we are doing better today. I counted 12 ships in sight today, there was one right ahead which we made up on in the forenoon, then there was a race all afternoon the other vessel trying to cross our bows and get ahead but she had to give it up. Then she went backward and went round our stern. Their captain seemed to be under the impression that he could beat us but he found out his mistake, for when we got her fairly behind us we set our skysail and ran right away from her at sunset. She was not to be seen. This vessel was the Abergeldie of Aberdeen bound from London for Sydney. We were closer to this vessel than we have been to any since we left. Once she was so close her men were dancing to the music of the bagpipes which one of the single men on our ship was playing. We could cry to the men on board. When we were opposite them some of them held up a sheep as much as to say we have plenty of meat and you haven't but we got equal with them as one of our sailors held up a rope for to give them a pull. We have a fine wind and have done a fine days sailing. We have got up all our extra sails now. Today there was a piece added to the mainmast and another sail stuck up called a staysail and there were other sails stuck up in places where I never imagined they could be put. When the canvas is up now there is 30 sails which ought to do us some good if we were only lucky enough to get good winds, but we have given up hopes now of making a quick passage.

Sunday 29th October

This Sunday is like all the rest we have had at sea. It is pretty rough but as the wind is fair and we are sailing well we don't mind. We passed muster as usual about 10 a.m., and the service after, then the bible class about 3 o'clock and another service at night. About 8 p.m. when the service was going on we got a fright the like of which I never will forget. In the morning we sighted a vessel ahead but we did not gain on her till dark when with a change of wind we were not long in running up alongside. The man on the lookout hung out a light on the starboard bow but it was only at the third shout and a red light on the starboard bow that the mates attention was drawn to it and when he saw it he raised his hands and said My God it's a red light too. Whatever was the reason we don't know but the strange ship was bearing down upon us full speed and seemed as if we should be cut in two. We just managed to get past her but so close that her jib boon passed over our poop. We now began to breathe fully and thinking we were too close to such a dangerous customer, but we were to be disappointed as she no sooner got hauled up than down she came again. We could not understand such proceedings. I was beginning to remember stories of pirates and much like. The mate said he thought she was determined to get a look at our name on the bows she was keeping so close to us. At any rate down she came in the dark like a great shadow. This time we could not avoid a collision but when she was close to us we close hauled our ship up against the wind so that when she did come down she missed us amidships but struck us near the bow tearing away our stansails and yards and some of the jib staysails and the whiskers boom and knocked two bulges in the side of the ship and breaking some of the railing on the forecastle. What with the screaming of the women and the cursing of the sailors and the crash of the falling spars and ropes we were in one sore plight. Our Captain evidently thought we would have come worse off as he had men stationed at the boats to let them go at a moments notice. However the stranger whoever she was paid for her capers as she lost her mizzen mast and half of the main mast. On board the Shenir nobody got a scratch but there was some anxiety concerning a number of women that had fainted and showed no signs of returning consciousness. We thought we were doomed this night as the strange ship had no sooner cleared away than there was a squall came down on us and we not being prepared for it after the hubbub we had been in, we had a busy hour of it getting the sails put right. Every man working with a will to get her brought too but it was not until there had been a sail blown away. When the squall cleared away we had to steer clear of another emigrant ship before us. She was running away down in the direction of the vessel that ran into us. I was glad when the night was over. Some of the passengers I believe will not recover from the shock during the whole voyage. Our Captain and Mates behaved very well and was much thought of for their smartness. I am thankful to God who brought us safe through all. I give here lines composed on the escape of the Shenir by one of the young girls. I got it from her sweetheart who was one of the single men Constables:

Twas on the 21st September/ In the year Eighteen Eighty Two
We left the shores of Bonnie Scotland/ A foreign land to view
Our barque sailed smooth and lightly/ Till in Africas sunny clime
We got a shock that made us shudder/ And our prayers to heaven ascend

Our hearts were light as usual/ Some laughing others sad
The night outside looked dull and drear/ And darkness wore her shroud
When all at once Oh Merciful/ A ships red light we saw
Death stared us blankly in the face/ A prayer did rise from all

Oh God have mercy on our souls/ Was heard from one and all
Strangers to prayer fell on their knees/ To spare their wicked lives
Our Captain heaven bless him/ And prosper him through life
For he did his duty nobly/ On that remembered Sunday night

When we heard him pleading wildly/ The stranger for us off to keep
He knew full well how many souls/ Seemed as lying at his feet

*And may prosperity attend him/ And the Mates and jolly
crew*
*And may they do their duty as nobly/ In their pilgrimage
all through*

*On the Monday morning after/ Sore heads and hearts
had some*
*Better an aching head on the Shenir/ Than breaking
hearts at home*
*Then heres to the old barque Shenir/ And heres to all our
mates*
*And heres to our darling old Captain/ For in gold he is
worth his weight*

*And heres to our precious Matron/ For she fills her duties
well*
*May the good Lord always guide her/ And be her friend
through life*

Built in 1869 for the Aberdeen to Australia trading route, this was a three masted wooden merchant sailing vessel owned originally by the Duthies. Dimensions: 218 x 39 x 21.

Although William comments throughout his diary on any ships sighted, this vessel seems to have received somewhat more attention than others. Clearly the "race" was fiercely contended, and it also seems that the crews were perhaps a little more excited and competitive than usual. Did the crew of the Abergeldie appear less disciplined than one might expect? The crew of the unidentified vessel displayed behaviour that could well have been the result of drunkenness; and this seems consistent with the crew of the Abergeldie very evidently making merry on their initial encounter. The following evenings terrifying experience as so vividly described led the crew and passengers of the Shenir to conclude that the unidentified vessel which almost collided with the Shenir, was likely the result of a drunken crew. These circumstances are at least suggestive that the unidentified vessel might have been the Abergeldie. Interestingly, some weight is added to this proposition when the ultimate fate of the Abergeldie is understood. In 1883 the Abergeldie appears as party to a court action in respect of "damages by collision"[28]. Again in October 1889, according to the Aberdeen Weekly Journal, she "collided with the barge ALDBOROUGH, off Barking, River Thames". The barge had rigging damaged and the ABERGELDIE grounded." And a month later in November 1889, the New South Wales Newcastle Morning Herald, reported of the Abergeldie that "she collided with a vessel whose name is unknown and foundered immediately" in the North Sea. She "was a regular wool trader to Sydney, and was well known for her fast passages under Captains Robertson, Crombie and Johnston". It may well be that many ships suffered collisions[29], and the Abergeldie certainly had history – but the identity of the offending ship remains a mystery.

---

[28] https://www.records.nsw.gov.au/state-archives/guides-and-finding-aids/vice-admiralty-court-of-new-south-wales-1787-1911/vice-admiralty-court-appendix-f
[29] More than 30 emigrant ships were lost in the 19th century : Shipwrecks on the UK Australian Run (oceans1.customer.netspace.net.au/austrun-wrecks.html)

Williams account of the near-disaster was subsequently described in the **Maryborough Chronicle on 3/1/1883:**

"A startling episode occurred on the 29th October, while the Shenir was in latitude 2 degrees north. While religious service was being conducted on board and engrossing every ones attention, a full-rigged ship, name unknown, sailed across the bows of the Shenir. The alarm was not given until a collision appeared imminent, whereupon Captain Stirling discontinued the service, and running on deck, gave orders to the steersman which saved the Shenir from running stern on to the stranger. As it was the vessels collided slightly, the Shenir sustaining the loss of a stansail boom, springing of the fore-royal mast, and carrying away of some of the back stays. The stranger was observed to receive more severe injuries, her mizzen top-gallant mast coming down with the run. The vessels quickly parted and proceeded on their respective roads, the stranger steering a northerly course. Fortunately no-one was hurt on board the Shenir, but nothing was known of the enemy, who volunteered no information, those on board confining their operations to swearing furiously."

Monday 30th October

The seamen are all busy today getting things put right. When the Captain came on deck after breakfast the girls on the poop gave him three cheers. The Captain says of all the escapes he has had at sea he never had such a narrow one as last night and says also it is due to a better and higher hand than his that we are all well and safe today. It is curious to hear the talk of a lot of the passengers about the other ship, all having different stories about what she was. Nobody can explain the conduct of the other ship as she ran in and out of our course. Certainly to look at her she seemed to have no object in view than to cut us in two and because she missed us the first time she turned about and tried it again. It is the belief today that both Captain and crew were drunk on board of the strange ship. Some of the passengers are afraid to go on deck today. Some of the passengers I heard tried to jump overboard but were held back, and thankful are they today. By sunset we have everything just right again and are sailing away as if nothing had happened. But for some nights there will be some anxiety and little sleep.

Tuesday 31st October

This day is pretty rough but we are sailing beautiful. Still the whole talk is about the collision and our narrow escape. For myself I am very thankful I am spared but I feel I could not explain myself on paper. Today we derived a little fun from the incident. One of the married men, an Irishman, was calling everybody stupid as he said he was quite sure if he had been on deck with a long pole he could have shoved the vessel off. The amusement and laughter we got off the man was good. The upshot of it was that we persuaded him to get away to bed after dinner and take a sleep, then get up and keep watch during the night. We also selected a long pole that he said would suit him and with this Big Jamie means to prevent collisions in the future. The Albatross made its first appearance today, one of them flying about the ship all day. Another thing we saw was the little nautilus sailing in the water. We tried hard to catch one with a bucket but didn't succeed. There was one sail in sight today. The weather feels colder. I believe we are past the equator but it has been kept quiet so that there would be no mischief on board. The Shenir is a teetotal vessel, so where there is no grog to be got the sailors never indulge in the old practice of rough shaving and such like. I heard since we have passed the equator today.

Rough Shaving

In the 19th century and earlier, the line-crossing (crossing the equator) ceremony was quite a brutal event, often involving beating first-timers (referred to as "pollywogs") with boards and wet ropes and sometimes throwing the victims over the side of the ship, dragging the pollywog in the surf from the stern. In more than one instance, sailors were reported to have been killed while participating in a line-crossing ceremony. On the second survey voyage of HMS Beagle, Charles Darwin, noted in his diary how he "was then placed on a plank, which could be easily tilted up into a large bath of water.

They then lathered my face & mouth with pitch and paint, & scraped some of it off with a piece of roughened iron hoop. A signal being given I was tilted head over heels into the water, where two men received me & ducked me. At last, glad enough, I escaped. Most of the others were treated much worse, dirty mixtures being put in their mouths & rubbed on their faces. The whole ship was a shower bath: & water was flying about in every direction: of course not one person, even the Captain, got clear of being wet through." [30]

There were 43 Irish people on board. Big Jamie was one of 6 married men named James, and although the ships passenger list does not in this case indicate the individuals nationality, an examination of the list suggests to a high degree of probability that the man referred to here was 39 year-old James Lappin, travelling with his wife Sarah and their 3 children. They most likely originated in Armagh, Northern Ireland.

Wednesday 1st November

Still the weather is not the best, the sea is coming over the forecastle and sometimes almost drowning us. Big Jamie was found last night at the foot of the main mast sound asleep, some of the sailors got a rope and tied him to the mast. Later on the mate

---

[30] Robert Fitzroy (1839) Narrative of the surveying voyages of His Majesty's Ships Adventure and Beagle between the years 1826 and 1836, London: Henry Colburn. pp. 57–58

found him and sent him down to his bed. Today we heard to our astonishment that we had a poet on board. One of the single men has a notice posted up that a copy of a poem on Sunday nights affair can be had at a penny each. I haven't seen it yet but I have heard plenty about it, and there is always a discussion whether it is poetry or prose. The young man that wrote it is the same one that got 6 days bread and water for writing to one of the girls. Our condenser broke down this morning and the water we got was very dirty as it came from the bottom of the tank and the weather is so warm we cannot do without it. I wish I could have a good drink of the Meldons[31] . Drink as much as you like of the ship water you are soon as dry as ever, it is not very good it is so warm. The ship is sailing splendid today and the only wish is that the wind will take us clear off the Cape which we intend to reach in 8 or 10 days.

William describes his 'astonishment' when he hears there is a poet aboard. In itself this expression is interesting – it points to an interest in literature, in addition to his already evident thirst for information. What appears strange is his reference to the debate among the passengers, whether the "poem" is poetry or prose, an unexpected topic in the context of steerage passengers in the late 19th century.

---

[31] *Meldons: Water from Meldon Burn, which rises in the Meldon Hills north west of Peebles town.*

Thursday 2nd November

Going splendid this morning with a south east wind. We are not exactly in our course, we are 2 points west of it. At daybreak we sighted a Dutch vessel ahead of us but before we went down for breakfast she was left far behind. Today we are passing the island of St Helena where Napoleon 1st was confined and died, but we cant see it. Our condenser is still at a standstill and our water today is disgraceful. The days and nights are beginning to change with us now. The days are getting longer while the days at home will be getting shorter.

Once the condenser broke down the only source of drinking water was from the barrels which had been filled from the reservoir at Loch Katrine. This water was almost invariably unpleasant – apart from the fact that it was untreated when it went into the barrels, which meant that over the following weeks, especially in warmer climates, bacteria would flourish, tainting both colour and taste and increasing the risk of gastrointestinal infection. It was also common for the barrels themselves to leach contaminates from earlier contents such as vinegar, wine and other products, into the water. Nor was Williams observation that "drink as much as you like of the ships water you are soon as dry as ever" just a result of the water temperature. Distilled water from the condensing machine is effectively demineralised, and one of the observed outcomes of humans drinking distilled water, apart from any health implications, is that thirst is not quenched to the same degree as with normal drinking water[32].

Friday 3rd November

The ship is still running a pretty stiff breeze, still from the S.E. I hear a good many of them who have been sleeping on deck complaining of having caught cold, they seem to forget we are not always to be in the tropics. At midday we passed a large ship homeward bound but she was too far off to be signalled too. In the evening the Salvation Army Captain held a thanksgiving service for our deliverance from a watery grave. Last Sunday night the meeting was very well attended as well it might.

Saturday 4th November

Still sailing splendid under the S.E. trade wind. There was a row this morning among the married men, some of them refusing to do some extra cleaning. The Doctor and Captain had both to be called before they got them to do it. I hear that we have been sailing this week about 200 miles per day. We consider this something good.

Sunday 5th Nov

The morning very dull with showers of rain. The bible class was held at 7 a.m. After muster we attended service when the Doctor made special mention of our

---

[32] Health Risks from Drinking Demineralised Water, Frantisek Kozisek, National Institute of Public Health, Czech Republic

By the 1860s the roles and responsibilities of the agents charged with the delivery of emigrants to their destinations were very well defined. On board ship the Captain was responsible for the crew and the safe passage of the vessel. The Doctor was responsible for the health and well-being, and the behaviour of the passengers. To assist him in the performance of his duties he appointed orderlies and constables from amongst the passengers to ensure the cleanliness of the environment, apportion the food rations, and to maintain discipline. Therefore any assault on a constable was in effect an assault on the Doctors official position, or as the Doctor put it, insulting the Queensland Government Constable, and would be punished accordingly.

Monday 6th Nov

Still raining very heavy this morning, any amount of fresh water for washing and plenty people willing to wash. About 9 a.m. we had another death on board, this time it was an infant 18 months old. It was buried during dinner time, the Doctor took the opportunity to bury it in quietness. The rain is stopped now but the sea is very rough. A sudden squall came down on us which broke the ropes of one of the sails and caused the ship to heel over so much that a number of women who were washing were sent tumbling over their buckets. One woman was lying on her back saying "Take me away, oh take me away". We had a good steady wind afterwards and we made the most of it. Tonight there is no moon but a star is shining with equal brightness to the moon.

Tuesday 7th Nov

We are still sailing under a very steady wind. There were two ships in sight today. In the afternoon we sighted one of them coming up behind us. And about 10 p.m. just when we were thinking of going to bed there was a shout, a light on the starboard bow. One nights experience was sufficient, the words were scarcely out of the mans mouth when we slewed round and gave her a wide berth.

Wednesday 8th Nov

This morning 5 a.m. we were awaked with the shout of "single men come up for your chests". We were not long in dressing and going on deck because it was now four weeks since we had been in them last. We were told also that we wouldn't get into them again until within a few days of landing. This was a big days nothing doing but opening and shutting boxes. Some of the married people grumbled because they would not get leave for the boxes up, but the Doctor ordered all boxes below which settled it.

Thursday 9th Nov

Got up very early this morning and saw a beautiful rising sun. We have every prospect of a good day and everything in our favour for good sailing. We signalled another vessel this morning which was the {Hawthorn?} from Newport belonging to Liverpool 58 days out and bound for the East Indies with a load of coal. In the forenoon the wind came on strong for our stansail boom, it went smash through the middle like a pipe shank although it was 12" thick. We could hear it cracking before it fell so we were all clear of it when it came down. It is the extra yard at the end of the fore yard, it projects over the side of the ship. There are two sails on it, one on the underside and the other on the top. The Captain is so determined to make the most of this wind that he ordered up another one in its place which was soon done, but it is bending pretty freely and we expect it down every minute. I saw a couple of pure white birds and one pure black and some beautiful speckled ones today. The black ones are what they call Cape Hens and the speckled ones Cape Pigeons. The squall has passed away and it is a beautiful night but very cold.

Friday 10th Nov

We have had a pretty fair nights sailing, but in the morning we are drifting with the tide and no signs of a breeze. The sky is clear and the sun is very hot. It is altogether a lively day but somehow I feel as if these nice days could be dispensed with for a good stiff breeze that would lay us down at Maryborough. We have had some good sailing lately and we cant be far from the Cape now. One of the ships we sighted on Tuesday is still in sight.

Saturday Nov 11th

A drizzly dirty morning. We have had another good nights sailing but when the sun rose the wind nearly left us. There is both a steamer and a sailing vessel in sight bit too far off to be signalled to. I saw a great big bird today, the sailors called it a Molly Hawk. It was followed by one a bit smaller and I think it must have been a young one as it didn't seem to be so strong in wing as the other one. The sea is beginning to rise making the ship roll very heavily. Down the forehatch among us there was one of the cupboards used for holding everything belonging to a mess. Once when the ship gave an extra heavy roll it was sent tumbling onto the floor. Everything was mixed up – there was pickles, currants, raisins, salt, pepper, mustard, tea, sugar and butter all lying mixed up. It was a good job it was near the end of the week, they will not have long to wait for a fresh supply of everything we get on Mondays. There was a woman fell today and broke her thumb. It is with the greatest difficulty we can manage to keep our feet. Many a time it has puzzled me to know how the youngsters manage it, in all sorts of weather they run about and play as if they were at home, and I have scarcely seen one of them fall. At 6 p.m. we had another of those rainy squalls which lasted 4 hours, the rain fell the whole time so hard that we thought it meant to rain this once and no more. At 7 p.m. there was another birth on board, a boy, he is to be called after the first mate. This makes the second birth.

Sunday 12th Nov

A gale has sprung up during the night and this morning it was still blowing with all its fury. There has been no sleep for the sailors last night and both watches are as busy as bees repairing the ropes and sails. At 8 a.m. one of the jib staysails broke loose and the first flap it gave it was sent into ribbons. They were in the act of taking in this torn sail when there was a crack overhead and on looking up there was one of the topsail yards broken through the middle and likely to come down at any moment. Another sail in a few minutes shared the same fate as the staysail and the largest sail of the lot, the mainsail, is blown full of holes. While we were at tea the ship gave a jerk and on going on deck to see what had happened, we saw the mainsail lying on deck, blown clean out of the ropes. Up on the yard there was a strip of canvas about 6 inches broad as if somebody had clipped off the sail. When the men were taking it away they had to lift it in small pieces. Today we have had a sample of what the wind can do.

Monday 13th Nov

Storm still continuing and another staysail has been blown to pieces. About 4 a.m. we had a heavy shower of hail. After breakfast when we were on deck there was plenty of work for us to do if we liked, pulling the ropes and such like, we like fine to get a haul at the ropes, it is fine exercise. I am getting tired doing nothing. The storm is increasing in fury and the waves are running up a fearful height. All the topsails are taken in. The whole day the ship has been rolling very heavily. This is another day I don't wish repeated. The vessel is turning so far on her side that sometimes we think she will go over altogether. At night the attempt was made to put the ship on a different tack but they couldn't manage it. Later on they made another attempt and succeeded but they had to take in all sail nearly. One of our cooks met with an accident today. He was walking along the deck carrying some water from the pump when he slipped his feet and was sent against the side of the ship, his legs getting jammed between the deck and a spare spar.

Thursday 14th Nov

Today is scarcely so stormy but the sea is running as high as ever. There are some of the waves coming on deck and making poor looking objects of us. The waves are so high that the tips of some of them go clear over the ship while the solid body of water falls on deck. The cook is confined to bed today his legs and feet have been so badly hurt yesterday. The baker in our mess has taken his place until he gets better. The Doctor today managed to get one of the Cape Pigeons, it is a pretty bird nicely speckled black and white. The sea is still very rough and as darkness sets in the wind is rising higher and higher. We expect a very rough night. We are sailing with only the foresail and 2 jib staysails and yet we are going at a great rate.

Wednesday 15th November.

While lying in bed last night I thought the sides of the ship were going to be smashed in, it was such a noise as the waves struck her. Every now and then there was a great flood of water came on deck with a great noise. We had another staysail carried away during the night, and at midday the chain of the fore yard gave way causing us some anxiety until it was properly secured for if it had come down it would most likely have killed somebody. As the day draws near a close the appearance of the sky is a little brighter and we think the storm is about blown past. I hear that someone from among the married people have fallen and broken their arm. It is a wonder there have not been more accidents because every few minutes in the day there is somebody sprawling on the deck. The water we are served with today is the Loch Katrine water we shipped at Glasgow. After lying in the tanks so long it is the colour of beer.

Thursday 16th Nov 100 miles

The sea has fallen a good bit during the night and the wind has almost left us. The ship is not going more than 4 or 5 knots an hour. The keeping up of our speed has a great effect on our spirits, when the ship is at a standstill or going slow we feel quite dull. The Doctor caught another Cape Pigeon today, they are a very pretty bird and they have a ruffle around their necks that anybody might {take} for her hat.

Friday 17th Nov   150 miles

The air is very cold. We have increased our speed a little today. We have a new fore top gallant yard made and fixed up in the place of the one that was broken down. We got a little exercise getting it brought forward, it was very heavy, it took about 20 of us to carry it. We are as weak as can be, we were all nearly done up with the short carry. We sighted the topsails of what appeared to be a full rigged ship away on our port beam sailing in the same direction we are but near night we are gradually leaving her behind.

Saturday 18th Nov 161 miles

It is very cold in the morning. We are still sailing very slowly and all things have been very quiet. The sailing vessel we saw yesterday is to be seen away astern today. I mentioned some days back about a poet we had on board, there are others. Two pieces appeared about our escape, one by a married man and the other by one of the single women. I will send the whole three and see what you think of them.

Sunday 19th Nov   125 miles

The wind is blowing from the S.E. so that we are continually going off our tack on to another. The weather is getting colder every day and today we had a forerunner of colder weather, a beautiful white bird with a long bill and black head and its tail forked like a swallows. The sailors call it an Ice Partridge and say it is seldom seen unless in extremely cold weather. It sat nearly all afternoon on the point of the jib boom but it was no use trying to catch it. Today there was one of the apprentices on board sent to the masthead and kept there for four hours for having been seen speaking to one of the single women. He didn't look much larger than some of the birds as he sat perched away up on the highest yard of the main mast.

Monday 20th Nov 141 miles

We could not sleep very well last night as we were surrounded by a thick fog and they were sounding the fog horn all night. We had another death on board, the first child born on board died this morning and was buried shortly after[33]*. The Doctor has laboured hard and long to catch an Albatross and today he succeeded in catching one. We all went aft to get a look at it and take its measure. It measured 8 ft 9" from tip to tip of the wing. The body is about the size of a swans and is almost pure white. Some of them flying about are a good deal larger than the one caught today. I saw a large whale spouting in the distance. The weather is very cold.*

Tuesday 21st Nov   146 miles

This morning the rain was falling very heavy and it is bitter cold with a good breeze. The birds that are

---

[33] The child who died was E.S.Barron, whose parents were George & Ellen.

flying about have increased in number today, there are flocks of each kind including Albatross, Cape Hens, Cape Chickens, Cape Pigeons, Mother Careys Chickens and Molly Hawks. The Cape Chickens are a small grey bird, they made their first appearance today and they are very swift on the wing. After tea the wind died away again.

Wednesday 22nd Nov   230 miles

This morning we were surrounded by a great shoal of whales, some of them of a great size and they were blowing away in every direction we liked to look. During the night the wind had risen to almost a gale. In the forenoon we had our flying jib sail blown away and the wind is still rising. It is blowing from the south west and the ship is plunging through the water nicely at a speed of 11 or 12 knots an hour. It is still very cold today, there are very few people on deck, the most of them preferring to stay below, but the young men must be up on deck to have their smoke no matter what the weather is like. I believe we have it colder here than you will have it at home or perhaps as coming so soon out of the heat will feel it more.

Thursday 23rd Nov   284 miles

We are still keeping up our speed, and the wind has changed, it is coming now dead behind us which makes the ship roll very heavily. About 7 p.m. there was a row among the young men. One of my

The rules extracted from British Passengers Act 1864

"the following shall henceforth be the rules for preserving order, for promoting health, and for securing cleanliness and ventilation, to be observed on board of every passenger ship proceeding from the United Kingdom to any port or place in Her Majesty's possessions…

• When the passengers are dressed, their beds shall be rolled up.

• The decks, including the space under the bottom of the berths, shall be swept before breakfast, and all dirt thrown overboard.

- The breakfast hour shall be from eight to nine o'clock, am. Before the commencement of breakfast, all the emigrants, except as herein before excepted, are to be out of bed and dressed, and the beds rolled up, and the deck on which the emigrants live properly swept.

- The deck shall further be swept after every meal, and after breakfast is concluded shall be also dry holystoned or scraped. This duty, as well as that of cleaning the ladders, hospitals, round houses, and water closets, and of pumping water into the cisterns or tanks for the supply of water closets, shall be performed by a party who shall be taken in rotation from the adult males above fourteen, in the proportion of five to every one hundred emigrants, and shall be considered as sweepers for the day. But the single women shall do all the necessary acts for keeping clean and in proper state their own compartment, where a separate compartment is allotted to them, and the occupant of each berth shall see that his or her own berth is well brushed out.

- On each passenger deck there shall be lit at dusk, and kept burning till daylight, three safety lamps, and such further number as shall allow one to be placed at each of the hatchways used by passengers.

- No naked light shall be allowed between the decks or in the hold at any time or any account.

- The scuttles and stern ports, if any, shall, weather permitting, be opened at seven o'clock, am., and kept open till ten o'clock, pm.; and the hatches shall be kept open whenever the weather permits.

• The coppers and cooking utensils shall be cleaned every day, and the cisterns kept filled with water.

• The beds shall be well shaken and aired on deck, weather permitting, at least twice a week.

• The bottom boards of the berths, if not fixtures, shall be removed and dry-scrubbed, and, weather permitting, taken on deck, at least twice a week.

• Two days in the week shall be appointed by the master as washing days; but no washing or drying of clothes shall be on any account be permitted between decks.

• On Sunday mornings the passengers shall be mustered at ten o'clock, am., and will be expected to appear in clean and decent apparel. The Lord's Day shall be observed as religiously as circumstances will admit.

• No loose hay or straw shall be allowed below for any purpose.

• No smoking shall be allowed between decks.

• The following kinds of misconduct are hereby strictly prohibited; that is to say, all immoral or indecent acts or conduct, taking improper liberties or using improper familiarity with the female passengers, using blasphemous, obscene, or indecent language, or language tending to a breach of the peace, swearing, gambling, drunkenness, fighting, disorderly, riotous, quarrelsome, or insubordinate conduct, also all deposits of filth or offensive acts of uncleanliness in the between decks; herein specified shall operate as a bar to any civil or criminal proceedings which may in the ordinary course of law be instituted for the same offence by any party aggrieved."

Friday 24th Nov   226 miles

Still sailing rapidly, a fair wind but the ship is rolling so much we can scarcely keep our feet. Some of us went aft this morning and saw our messmate. He opened the port and looked out but we could not get near enough to speak to him. He seemed to be quite happy, he was laughing away, he held up his hands and let us see the handcuffs on him, but shortly after that he got out after a night in irons. He says he was quite happy and comfortable, he had a fine bed. The first mate said today that if we had 20 days of this it would land us in Queensland but we cant expect the wind to last that time. We have taken down all the jib sails and staysails, the spanker and the gaff topsail. The ship is rocking fearful and the waves coming over the whole.............

At this point there is a gap in the diary between Friday 24th November and the 5th December. Family tradition has it that William was found to be consorting with a single girl on board ship, and received 10 days in irons.

5th Dec

When somebody is there with a match we make a rush and before the partys own pipe is lit there is a dozen all round him wanting a light from that one match. We are learning a fine lesson on economy. Just as it got dark today the wind fell a little and the sailors were ordered up aloft to set the skysail again. They wish this sail would blow down as it is such a height for them to climb.

Wednesday 6th Dec.

We are still sailing very fast. While I was writing this I got a fine laugh from one of my messmates. He said as he was writing he felt something pulling away at his papers. He could not think what it was till he saw a big mouse hanging on to the papers. (We have a good many of these gentlemen on board. I have kept very clear of them as yet). He tried to lift the paper but Mr Mouse wouldn't let go easily. He saw a stick lying under the table, when the louse saw him take it up he let the paper go and was preparing to run, but he caught him by the hind legs and ran upstairs with him and threw him overboard. He expects some passing ship will pick him up. There are some great hunts at night for them.

Thursday 7th Dec

Fine winds going well today. There is a good deal of amusement caused by a number of young men who drill on deck every morning. There is one man who is always in command and puts them through their pacings and then marches them round the deck two or three times. It usually finishes with a sham fight as a lot more of the men try to stop them as they march around the deck. It is laughable to hear the officers shouting out the words of command.

Friday 8th Dec

Very little wind today, we are not sailing very fast. A special service was held tonight in the forecastle as one of the sailors is very unwell. He is an old man, his name is O'Bryan. We made a collection for him a short time ago. The weather is getting warmer now.

Saturday Dec. 9th

It is a great deal warmer today, it is like a summer day at home. We are all making ourselves look decent for Sunday, some are shaving others are brushing their boots. I rose this morning at half past two and was up all the rest of the morning with another young man I have become acquaint with. We sat and wrote a while then went up on deck about 4 a.m. and had a walk around about and then went into the engine room and had a smoke. It was very pleasant sitting in front of the fire. It is not often we get near one, it brought us in mind of home. Then about 5 o'clock we got some hot water from the cook and had a cup of tea. I give here a list of our crew:

21 A.B. Seamen, 5 Ordinary Seamen

2 Emigrant Cooks, 1 Ship Cook, 1 Emigrant Baker,

2 Pursers, 1 Engineer, 1 Carpenter

1 Boatswain, 3 Apprentices, 2 Stewards,

2 Mates, 1 Doctor, 1 Matron And The Captain

It is a double crew, there will be only about 12 seamen coming back with it. They are bound to carry a double crew for some to man the boats if they are needed. There were some porpoises in sight today.

Sunday 10th Dec.

A splendid morning but not much wind. Passed muster at 10 a.m. then attended the usual service. About 12 the wind was stronger and sent us away at about 12 knots an hour. All the talk just now is about when we will be landed, everyone has his own story about how far we are off. As I said before we get no official notice of how we are getting on. It is of course all surmise.

Some say we are 3000 miles while others has it 1500 mile, that is a little difference of 1500 miles in their accounts. We had the bible class between decks at 3 p.m., the subject was Christ the Light of the World. And then the meeting at night, it was too cold to have it on deck so it was held down in the married quarters. We sighted a ship today a great distance off, it very soon was out of sight.

Monday 11th Dec

I had to be up this morning to be on the lookout for provisions as it was my mess week along with another mate, so we are never sure of a minute when they will be crying out "Single Men for Flour" or something else. It is a very disagreeable morning it was so wet, keeping us mostly between decks but we are sailing very well. There were a number of porpoises about the ship today. There was a good deal of seaweed floating about making us think that we were near land. Everybodys talking about when we will be landed, some of them betting that we will be landed before Xmas. The old sailor that is so bad was moved to the hospital today. There is one of our mess very bad with asthma. He has been complaining nearly all the voyage. He takes very little food. He is a man of about 30 years of age.

Tuesday 12th Dec

Rose at 5 a.m., had a drink of coffee which was very nice. Tis not so cold now as it was, but it is still very cold in the morning and at night. It is light about 3 or 4 in the morning and not dark till near 8 at night, so it makes a long day. It will be nearly the opposite at home. We are going fine with a fair wind, there is little rain today. The man that was bad in our mess was taken to the hospital. Today he is very bad, I don't know what he will do when we get to Queensland as I think he is getting worse every day. Later just after dinner as Jim Layton and I was going along the deck one of the constables came forward to us and told us he was dead. We were very much struck it was so sudden, he being amongst us such a short time ago. He was up on the deck when the Doctor came down for his usual inspection and one of the constables told him he was getting no better so the Doctor told him to take him aft and he would see if he was bad enough to go into the hospital. That was nearly 11 o'clock and about 1 he was dead, then buried about 4 p.m. It was very solemn he being amongst us five short hours before being cast into the deep. The Doctor says he thought he was better because he did not come up for his medicine. There are some condemning the Doctor very severely for not giving him proper nourishment as he could hardly eat any of the meat when he came on board. At first he was very cheery but he never looked very well. He always said he would be all right if he was just landed and then he said " After I have made a bit of money I will send for the lassie" but alas poor Dick. That is the first death down our hatch and we have lost one out of our number of mess. His name was Richard Davidson[34].

Wednesday Dec 13th

There was a fine breeze this morning. When the log was heaved at 8 a.m. we were going at 9 knots an hour and when it was heaved at 4 p.m. we were going at 9 and a half knots, and it is still keeping up the speed. The log is heaved every two hours. There

---

[34] Richard Davidson, born 1854, Montrose, Scotland. Parents William and Alexandrina

was a woman got a very severe fall tonight as she and her husband were stepping on to the hatch, he fell forward and she fell back over. She had a child not long ago. At the bible class tonight there was special mention made about Richard Davidson, it was a very solemn and touching meeting. The Salvation Army Captain spoke very well. And one of the married men that was there spoke very feelingly about parting with friends at home that we might never see again. It carried my thoughts back to home and all the friends I had left in Scotland.

Thursday Dec 14th

Rose about 6 o'clock, it was a fine morning, we have a fair wind but light. This is the time of day by the bells, 8 bells 12 o'clock, 1 bell half past, 2 bells 1, three bells half past 1, four bells 2, five bells half past 2, six bells 3, 7 bells half past 3, eight bells 4, nine bells half past 4 and so on. The day is divided into 4 hours. The bell is hung in the forecastle with a piece of rope on the tongue then one of the sailors strike the number of strokes for the time of the day. The condensing engine was stopped today so that is one sign we are getting near our destination. The woman that fell yesterday is all right, I saw her going about tonight.

Friday 15th Dec

It was very calm today, not much wind, not for us anyway. It is very wearisome going so little and so near landing. I think we are going up the near coast of Tasmania. We were to go by the South of it and we were sailing to the north today so we are not so very far off Maryborough now but there is so many stories. Some say we were to go through Basses Straits that is between Australia and Tasmania. But I think it is the south of Tasmania that we have sailed. There was a land bird flying about today and another Albatross caught.

Saturday 16th Dec

When I went up on deck this morning we were going at a great speed. The wind had risen through the night. It is getting worse and worse. Sail after sail was taken in until we are nearly under bare poles and it is blowing us off course. One of the jib sails was carried away. One of the spars on the foremast sprung so the sailors had to go away up the rigging and lash a small spar across it. The sailors had a very rough job of it today, both watches were our together 2 or 3 times reefing the sails, about a score of them running up the rigging close at one anothers heels. There were some very heavy seas coming over the side today, there were some got wet from head to foot. I got a small part of one of them. I have been very lucky. I think it has been blowing harder today than it has done since we left. It is a great change from yesterday. There was another death on board, a young child about a year old. We had boiled beans to our dinner instead of pea soup. They were not bad. I think I could eat anything now. We get plenty meat.

Sunday 17th Dec

We had a terrible night of it down below, we could get no sleep with the noise of presses falling with their contents and forms and tin dishes rattling about. I rose about 6 o'clock but could not find my boots until after a long search when I found them about six berths off. Then I went upon deck and found we were sailing along splendid with a fair wind. It was not so strong as yesterday but still it was a strong wind. It pleased us fine as it was sending us on in the right direction. After a while I went down below where two of my messmates and I had a tin of coffee. I was nearly done with mine when the ship gave a rock which sent me along the seat on to the floor at a great speed but that was the least of it as the flour for the Sunday duff was in a wooden dish on the table when away it went off the table on to the floor alongside me. I got a fine lot of it about me but that was nothing. It was the loss of the flour that was troubling us, but we managed to gather the most of it up again. We watched it better after that. We expect it to be a grand one today as we have kept all weeks currants and raisins for it so there is plenty of fruit in it but I will see what it is like when it comes down. I am writing this the time when we are waiting on it being ready. There was no muster, we have never seen the Doctor neither yesterday or today. A little while ago I was standing at the side of the ship looking over when the ship lurched that much that the water came rushing over the side. If I had been about 3 yards further along I would have got a proper dip. I escaped with very little but some of them standing at the other side of the deck got a right dip. As the ship coming up again the water that was on the deck was sent rushing against the other side drenching them to the skin that were standing there. Our duff was a great success, it was splendid, it was fair black with currants and raisins. We had the bible class as usual between 3 and four in the afternoon. There was no service on deck today. One of the staysails was blown away.

Monday 18th Dec 226 miles

We have a fine breeze and going on fine. The sea is not so rough today. I have nothing particular to mention but I give here the number of emigrants on board. There is 86 single girls 44 married couples that is 88 men and women and 103 single men.

Tuesday 19th Dec 267 miles

The wind rose today to a great height, it began a little after breakfast and rose higher and higher. The sea also rose to a great height in a very short time but we thought little of it as it was sending us on in the right direction. Both wind and sea were driving us on and sail after sail had to be taken in. We had only 3 sails up and 1 staysail and still going at the rate of 12 miles an hour.

Wednesday 20th Dec   230 miles

Still going along at a great rate with a fair wind. Wind and sea are driving us on, we have hopes of being landed next week. We had the meeting down below this evening between 7 and 8. It was very solemn as it will most likely be the last wed meeting we will have on board not to say we will be landed but we will be in such a bustle. The Salvation Army Captain and the young purser spoke with much feeling. There was one of the single men got put in irons tonight for fighting. Another fellow and him quarrelled about the soft bread. There were two of my messmates had a fight today. There are some great rows, we have had two or three in our mess. We have got the name of the "34 Warriors". All the messes are numbered, and 34 is the number of ours.

Thursday 21st Dec 152 miles

Sailing along fine with a strong wind. We have done some good sailing the last day or two but it is very disagreeable on deck, everything is wet with the waves coming over. Heard today we had broke the thousands[35] and we're into the hundreds now so that is something. We are wearying very much to be landed as the voyage is getting tedious, every day is so much alike. All the talk now is when will we be landed now. Everyone has his story but everyone is of the opinion we will be landed before the new year. The young man that was in irons got out this

---

[35] Less than a thousand miles to their destination

morning. The Captain sighted land today with his glass but we could not see it. About 8 p.m. the wind fell altogether, but after there arose a light breeze blowing at intervals but we were hardly moving.

Friday 22nd Dec

I could not sleep last night for the rocking of the ship so got up about 12 p.m. and went on deck and had a smoke. We were nearly becalmed at that time so after a walk around I came down and had a read at a book belonging to the library. I was enjoying myself very much when the light went out and I could not get another. It appears that the supply of candles are failing so I went on deck again. We were sailing a little better after a while. I came down and tumbled into my bunk with my clothes on. I rose again about six and went up on deck and found we were going along at a good rate under a pretty stiff breeze. It was reported today that we would see land about night but we never saw it.

Saturday 23rd Dec.   140 miles

We have been sailing along splendid today but we are a little off our course. It has been a great talk this day or two among the Englishmen whether we would get anything extra for Monday it being xmas day, but today we got an extra allowance of flour and raisins so it will be duffs and buns on Sunday and Monday to all intents and purposes. The single woman had an amateur theatrical performance tonight. There were

A complaint or petition critical of the Doctor could
have been costly. As a Government appointed
officer, in addition to his normal day to day salary, he
received a bonus payment at the end of the journey
which was based on a satisfactory report from the

passengers, the Immigration Inspector and the Captain. The bonus was set at 10 shillings per passenger, so was a major part of his annual remuneration. However in reality, unless there was a complete breakdown in order, or an unavoidable issue such as a catastrophic outbreak of disease that could not be hidden, the payment scheme was structured in such a way that the Doctor and the Captain depended on each on others support to maximise their pay. The Captain was, on foot of a similar report, typically paid 50% at the outset of the voyage, and 50% on delivery. So it was always unlikely that a Captain would side with the passengers in opposition to a Doctor.

Sunday 24th Dec   190 miles

Sailing along fine with a fair wind which kept up all day. Has muster at 10 and the service from the Doctor which consisted of reading sermon and prayers and singing which was the best of it. In the afternoon between 2 and 4 there was a meeting conducted by the young purser who spoke on the resurrection, he spoke very well. At night there was another meeting on deck between 7 and 8 conducted by the Salvation Army Captain. He spoke splendid on the judgement. He was very serious, he said it would be the last time he would speak to us all together. The whole of the meetings were held on deck today at the poop, so the girls were at them all. They got down to the service in the morning but were at the poop at the rest of them, but they could hear fine.

Just before the close the matrons whistle sounded so they had to go below, they have to be kept pretty close.

Monday 25th Dec Xmas day   191 miles

We have a splendid day, the sun shining, and we are sailing along well under a fair wind. A different day to what you will have at home, you will most likely have snow and cold, we have sunshine and heat. We had a fine pie for our dinner made with preserved meat and a paste over it, and at teatime we had shortbread and cakes so it was something like Xmas day. There was a sacred concert at night by the choir conducted by the Salvation A. Captain but it was partly a failure. The cause of it was they put up a rope to keep the single men from coming too close. It caused an ill feeling. It looked as though they did not want us there at all, so there was a dance started a little further forward and allowed to go on. We tried a concert of our own but were ordered to stop as we were making too much noise. After the concert there were some prizes given to the school children. Just as they were finishing the lookout reported a sail on the port bow. There was a great rush to the side of the ship as most thought it was land he cried out. That is the only ship we have seen this good while. After the concert the young purser had a religious meeting. After he had been speaking a good while and was done, some of the sailors and passengers began to sing songs such as Rise Jock Rise. After they had sung awhile the steward and some of them began to sing hymns quite near where the others were singing, so after a while the steward jumped up on a form and began to speak. Some of the sailors were singing a song, and the rest the chorus. When the chorus was done and not so much noise he cried out to the sailor that was singing if he did not stop God would strike him down, if not now at some other time. I think it was very much out of place for him to speak that way. When the meeting was going on there was no noise at all and he was listened to with every attention. It has caused a bad feeling against him. There were great arguments on religious subjects all night.

The S.A.Captain says it was not with his consent the rope was put there at all. The Doctor was presiding over the concert, it is the same on Sunday mornings when the Doctor conducts it. When the Sal.A.Capt or the young purser have a meeting on deck there is no rope and there is more quietness without it than with it. The sailors had a holiday today. There was a deputation of married women went to the Doctor today and asked for the single girls to have the liberty to come on deck. It was a fine laugh to see the Doctor among them, they all closed round about him and he could not get away. When he saw he was fixed he said he would go and see what the matron said about it. So they let him go see the matron but she would not let them, so it was of no use, the girls had to stay where they were.

Rise Jock Rise[36]

Rise, Jock, rise, Jock, d'ye no hear the bells - they're ringin'?

Lyin' sleepin' in yer bed, I'm shair ye cannae thrive.

Early in the mornin', I hear my auld wife cryin,

"Jock, are ye waukent, for it's half past five?"

Rise, Jock, rise, Jock d'ye no hear the bells a-ringin?

Mind ye're no bidin wi yer Mammy noo.

I'll gang an' leave ye if ye dae me ill,

So rise, Jock, rise, Jock, there's the hauf-oor bell.

Rise, Jock, rise, Jock, rise and light the fire, Jock, mak a cup o tea.

When ye have it made, Jock, hand it ower tae me.

Before ye ging tae yer work, Jock, kiss your duckie, do,

And maybe some time efter that I'll dae the same for you.

---

[36] Music notation by Aidan Cronin, Song by J.C.MacDonald, a notable concert hall comic in the late 19th century.

Tuesday 26th Dec   216 miles

We have still a fair wind which is blowing very steady and sending us along splendid. The sailors were busy this morning getting the anchor chains hauled out and fixed on to the anchor so we cant be far off our destination. Some of the other sailors were washing the bulwarks and other parts of the ship today, and the cooks were getting the galley washed out. And our place has to be washed today and has to be washed every day now until we land. All the beds were up on deck today, there were a great many of them thrown overboard, mine among the rest. I could hardly carry it, I was afraid of it going into pieces. I had a big knot at one end of it where it had burst so instead of sewing it I tied a knot on it to keep in what stuff was left of it, so they are just as well overboard for all the time we will have. The bible class was held tonight, it was a grand meeting. After it was over Mr McAllister, the young purser was presented with his testimonials by one of the single men who spoke very well. The young purser was quite taken by surprise but he returned thanks with much feeling, after which the Salvation A. Captain and others made some very appropriate remarks.

Wednesday 27th Dec   236 miles

We have always a good steady wind and going along at a fine rate. We expect to be anchored tomorrow so we are drawing near the end of our voyage at last. We sighted 2 ships today and about dinner time everyone was on the lookout for land. We could see what the sailors called land, it was just like a black cloud. About five o'clock we could see it was land quite well, that is our first sight of Queensland. At night we were going at the rate of 11 knots an hour so that will soon bring us to our desired haven. There was a great noise tonight below. A lot of the single men were tearing up their beds and throwing the stuff all over the place. In a short time the floor was all covered as if there had been a fall of snow. There were some in their beds, they were in a fine mess, the other fellows covering them as they slept. The Doctor came down and told the constables to take the names down of those who made any more noise.

Thursday Dec 28th   101 miles

I was up all night with one of my messmates whose bed is over the side along with mine. We sat and wrote and read and had hot tea, then another walk on deck and a smoke. Then we lay down till the morning and had a sleep for a short time. I enjoy being up on deck through the night, it is fine. The anchors were hung over the side today all ready for letting go. We saw a lighthouse with a revolving light, it was quite distinct. I suppose it is at Sandy Cape that is at the north end of Sandy Island. That is the way we are going in down Hervey Bay between Sandy Island and Queensland. We are keeping some of the sails down as the Captain does not want to go in until daylight tomorrow.

Great Sandy Island (now Fraser Island) is located along the southern coast of Queensland. At c.75*15 miles, the island is considered to be the largest sand island in the world. Sandy Cape lighthouse is located on Sandy Cape, the most northern point on Fraser Island, Queensland. It was built in 1870, and would have looked much the same to William as we see it here.

The lighthouse seen from the front of the lighthouse keepers' cottages,1907

Friday 29th Dec   *42 miles*

At daybreak we began to sail into the bay against a headwind. In a short time we began to see land on each side of us, it is a strange looking coast, the trees are growing quite close to the waters edge. There was great excitement on board, the sides of the ship were quite covered with people looking at their future home. We got opposite Woody Island and tacked backward and forward to get in. When it came dark we saw two lights one on each side of the entrance. Just a little after we saw a steamer going in. We had signals flying nearly all day but we were not noticed until nearly 4 p.m. After dark the Captain sent up some rockets. We cast anchor about 10 p.m.

Saturday 30th Dec

We raised anchor about 4 a.m. At last we have seen a Queenslander. The Pilot came on board this morning about 2 o'clock. He came in a little boat. He cried out if there was any disease on board and the mate cried all well but he would not come on board until he asked the Doctor. So the Doctor had to be raised out of bed, then the Pilot asked him if there was nothing wrong. The Pilot is a big strong looking man, he is a great {swell[37]}. He brought a lot of papers on board with him. Everyone that had a paper had a great crowd around him listening to the news. I got a read of one, it was the Maryborough Chronicle. There was very little in it. It was dated 20th

---

[37] Victorian slang for well dressed.

December. I saw in it that Mr Gladstone had resigned the Chancellorship of the Exchequer and that Arabia Pasha had got banished. I have missed the papers very much. It will likely be in the papers today or tomorrow that we have arrived but we are still on board beside Sandy Island. We have dropped anchor just about 300 yards off it. I expect we will be here till the Inspector comes on board. The island is well named for it is a sandy place. We can see people walking on the shore quite plain. We gave them a hurrah. They were waving their hats and throwing them up in the air. We can see 4 wood houses on the shore. I hear that if there had been any trouble on board we would have been put ashore here as it is the quarantine station. We saw 2 or 3 ships today, there was a steamer passed very close to us, we gave it a cheer which was returned. There was some great cheering and singing tonight after we cast anchor at 5 p.m. Cheers were given for all the parties on board except the Doctor and Constables who got groans instead. There was some very good singing going on. The old sailor who was unwell died today, he will be taken ashore and buried tomorrow.

Just days before William embarked on his long voyage to Australia, one story making the headlines in Britain was the nationalist uprising in Egypt. This uprising had been brewing for several years and was an attempt to remove Egypt from the influence of foreign powers particularly Britain and France. Amongst Britain's many vested interests, one was maintaining

control of the Suez Canal (Britain had since 1875
been the majority shareholder in the company that
had developed the canal back in the 1860s). On the
13th September 1882 the leader of the revolt, Arabi
Pasha (pictured), was defeated at Tel-al-Kebir. While
William travelled to Australia, Arabi Pasha was tried
under court martial for sedition in early December.
He was sentenced to death, though the sentence
was subsequently reprieved. His exile to Ceylon was
big news.

Sunday 31st Dec

*The sailor who died yesterday was taken ashore and
buried this morning, the flag was half-mast high all
day. When they came back they brought a lot of
branches off the trees, there was a great rush for
them. I got some leaves which I will send home. It is
very dull today and some rain. We have been
expecting a steamer all day with fresh provisions, it
has not come. I suppose the Inspector will be on
board tomorrow. About 4 p.m. two natives came off*

Sandy Island in a boat, it was the strangest looking boat I ever saw. It was flat bottomed, it was shaped just like the wooden frames for framing an arch. They had very poor oars, their row locks was just part of a tree like a catapult. They were strange looking beings with long matted hair. They are not very big. They brought some fish which they exchanged for biscuits and tobacco. About dark there were others, two came up, but they were not allowed to come on board as the meeting was going on. There were 3 or 4 ships near us today. There are 4 anchored near us.

Maryborough Chronicle (MC) 1/1/83

"The immigrant vessel Shenir arrived at its anchorage at the White Cliffs yesterday (Sunday) morning. The reports to hand are very meagre. We are informed that one or two deaths have occurred during the voyage, and at present there are two cases of sickness on board. Dr Power (the Health Officer), Mr North (the immigration agent) and other officials will be conveyed to the vessel this morning by the steamer Derwent, leaving here about {4} o'clock. Arrangements are being made for the steamship Ranelagh to bring up the immigrants either this evening or tomorrow morning."

Monday 1st Jan 1883   *New Years Day*

We are spending our new year on board as we have not yet a steamer to take us up to Maryborough. We are still anchored off Sandy Island. The natives have been going backward and forward all day bringing fish shells and flowers and changing them for biscuits blankets tins tobacco and anything you like to give them. One of them brought a woman with him. She was all dressed up with feathers stuck in her hair. The Inspector came down about 10 a.m. today with some more people on a steamer, they brought fresh beef and vegetables. We had some in our pea soup today, it was a great treat, and then we had the beef to our tea, ¾ pound each. After the Inspector had walked through the ship he called the roll. He brought the letters on board. I got two one from Mr Neilson Gympie [38] and one from Jim Thomson and a note, saying there was a registered letter lying at Maryborough, which I have to present at the Post Office when I will get the letter, and he also told me there was another one for which there was a shilling to pay. Mr Neilson said in his letter he would be at Maryborough to meet me if he knew when we would be in. If not to telegraph to Gympie and tell him when we arrived, and to come with the first tram which I intend to do. They are very kind. Just a little after the Inspector came on board there was a steamer passed close to us with an excursion party on board going to Sandy Island. We gave them a good cheer which was returned. As it was coming back in the evening one of the passengers on board of it cried out "Single Men

---

[38] Gympie - famous for its gold rush since the 1840s. In approx. 1880 Hamilton Neilson from Peebles, Scotland left with his young wife Anne (Prosser) and baby to take part in the gold rush. He mined gold at Gympie. He returned to Scotland towards the end of the century, and lived at Gympie, St Andrews Road, Peebles through the first World War.

*for Burgoo". That is the name we have for porridge. I
expect he has been on an emigrant ship. There were
some of the emigrants on the shore today, they got
hold of a boat which some of the excursionists had
who came on board of our ship and while they were
going through it the emigrants took off with it to the
shore. The men couldn't get off until they came back.
One of the ships boats also took some on shore. The
Inspector brought a Cingalese on board with him, he
is very black and features like a woman and long hair
rolled up at the back of his head. Where we are lying
it is full of sharks, we can see them moving about,
any person falling overboard would not have much
chance of their life. The petition which was filled up
and signed was handed to the Inspector today. I
don't know what will come of it.*

2/1/83 MC   Vessel in harbour   Shenir

"We are informed that the immigrants by the ship
Shenir will be brought up to town about 2 o'clock
this afternoon in the steamer **Liechardt** which leaves
the wharves at 4 o'clock this morning, Dr Power the
Health Officer went down to the vessel yesterday
morning in the s. Derwent and after careful
examination granted the usual pratique. It was
arranged by the local agents for the Ranelagh to
bring up the "new chums" yesterday afternoon, but
owing to some inadvertence in the despatch or
delivery of a telegram, the Ranelagh passed without
being signalled for the above purpose, therefore the

new arrivals were debarred from spending their New Year's Day on shore."

The "Leichardt"[19] was an iron paddle steamer of 459 tons, was built at Pyrmont, Sydney in 1864/5 running between Sydney, Brisbane, Maryborough and Rockhampton .

Turned in last night on to the boards and slept well, awoke about four and woke up one of my messmates and had a tin of coffee. Just before breakfast there were two steamers came in sight, We were all wondering whether they were coming to our ship or not some saying one think, some another. But we were soon put out of our suspense as they both steamed alongside, and then there was a great cheer. One of them was for some provisions, it was an old steamer for towing timber. There were Cingalese on board of it, the same as the one we had on board. The sailors lowered the one that was on our ship on to it but just as it was leaving he came up a rope on board of us again. The other one was the one to take the emigrants up to Maryborough. We had a fine rush, we had our breakfast to get, and the boxes to come up out of the hold for us to get ourselves changed and then put on the steamers. After we had got on board the rope men cast off and then we left the good ship Shenir which had been hour home for so long. We gave her a right good hearty cheer, the Mate and crew cheered us as we left. We had the Captain on board of the steamer. There were no passengers left on the Shenir except

Maryborough Harbour

Having spent 3 months in uncomfortable conditions on board ship, for William to describe conditions on arrival as "rough" suggests a pretty dismal state of affairs. This was echoed in the local news on 4/1/83:

"The newly arrived immigrants by the vessel Shenir have evidently to put up with greater discomfort than any of their predecessors in the local immigration barracks. Undoubtedly the unfavourable weather ever since they set foot on land will have added to their little troubles and annoyances, but the arrangements for their accommodation in the depot seem to be deplorably incomplete. First impressions of a town or people frequently cling, and when it is known that there are no blankets or beds allowed by the Government for the young men, it will seem to them that due attention has not been paid to their comfort after a long sea voyage. We have several times pointed out that the arrangements at the immigration barracks are not quite calculated to display that feeling of welcome and hospitality to which Australians, as a rule, honestly lay claim. The approaches and surroundings of the depot are positively miserable, knee deep in mud, more like a pigsty than anything else, hardly the proper condition of a place leading to the temporary domicile of our new countrymen. About 100 newcomers succeeded in making engagements, chiefly as farm labourers or domestic servants. The wages of the single man averaged from £30 to £45 a year with rations; and of married couples from £60 to £75; and the single girls obtained 7s to 10s per week".

3/1/83 Maryborough Chronicle

"The Barque SHENIR, having reported at the customs, consignees are required to present Bills of Lading and pay freight and charges without delay. Captain Stirling will not be responsible for any debts contracted by his crew without his written authority./ Shipping News   - Entered in: Shenir,.....with 376 immigrants and cargo, John Walker & Co, agents. / Imports: Ex Shenir:........289 bags salt; 250 cases whiskey; 130 cases cement; 3191 cast iron pipes; 30 cases galvanised iron; 86 kegs rivets; 12 boilers; 339 iron plates; 6 cases leather belting; etc."

3/1/83 P.2 Local News

"The urgent necessity for some improved method of administering the pilot service of this harbour is shown in the case of the immigrant ship SHENIR. This vessel came into Herveys Bay during thick weather on Friday and during the afternoon was beating about off the Fairway Bouy signalling for a pilot. She received a response from the signal station at Woody Island but could not read the flags. Eventually the Shenir anchored for the night and the Captain, being in strange waters, continued signalling by means of rockets. It was not until early next morning that the pilot boat found her way to the Fairway, and pilot Evans was put on board the ship. No doubt the pilot cutter and her crew, including the pilot on duty, have their time fully, though owing to the neglected state of the port, improperly employed in replacing the makeshift beacons which are allowed to do duty and are constantly disappearing. ….It is an iniquitous thing that a ship with over 400 souls on board should be compelled to go cruising among the dangerous shoals in Herveys Bay for even a single hour without the assistance of a pilot."

3/1/83 P.4

"The immigrant ship having shown a clean bill of health and received pratique[40], her human freight was discharged yesterday. The A.S.N.Co's steamer Leichardt proceeded to the anchorage at the White Cliffs at daylight and the transhipment of the 370 and odd souls being effected under the superintendence of Mr.Smyth, immigration agent, and Captain Cottier, the steamer moved away from the ship. The weather up to this proved tolerably fine, but rain then fell, and when the immigrants reached the wharf the elements were very badly behaved, the new arrivals having to submit to a very damp reception on landing. There was nothing approaching a demonstration, and under the guidance of Mr Ranger, the wardsman, they were marched to the barracks and there housed as comfortably as the accommodation therein permitted. The hiring of servants will commence at 9 o'clock this morning. The immigrants were under the charge of Dr. J.G.Praddle who proved a strict disciplinarian, and had an able coadjutress in the

---

[40] License given to a ship to enter port on assurance from the captain to convince the authorities that she is free from contagious disease

matron, Mrs Simons. The health of the immigrants was good, a result no doubt partly due to the roomy nature of the ship. Eight deaths took place during the voyage, the victims being all young children. Four births are also recorded. The Shenir left Glasgow on 22nd September and had baffling winds for some time before picking up the trades. She crossed the equator on 31st October, passed the meridian of the Cape of Good Hope on (23rd?) November, enjoyed westerly winds to the Australian coast and then had fair weather till reaching Breaksea Spit. She anchored off the Fairway Bouy on 29th December, 98 days out from Glasgow. She spoke to the Inchmaurn[41] and Abergeldie, ships bound for Sydney, also a vessel from Liverpool bound for Honolulu, 45 days out.

The Shenir is a splendid vessel, nearly new, of very handsome design. She is an iron ship and belongs to the "Mountain" line of Messrs Smith & Service, London. She brings a large cargo for Maryborough, and is consigned to the agency of Messrs John Walker & Co."

Wednesday   3rd Jan

After breakfast which consisted of beef and bread and tea went to the emigration office and asked if I would get a pass to Gympie. The agent said yes but said I was to go and ask as many as I knew who were going, so I went and got some. We went to him and got the ticket and got our boxes down to the station

---

[41] Inch Murren

and left about 5 p.m. for Gympie. Jim Layton and some of the young men came down to see me off. I was very sorry to part with them all. When we arrived at Gympie, Hamilton Neilson {left another} to meet me. I knew him at once. He shook hands and welcomed me to Queensland, so we went away to his house. Mrs Neilson was waiting on us, I got a splendid reception. I will now close my diary and hope you are all pleased with it. I am thankful to God who has brought me safe through all.

Diary Ends

42

---

[42] Gympie Goldfields: Queensland State Archives, Digital Image ID 5115 Copyright expired.

QUEENSLAND
Gympie Goldfield

"The immigrants of the Shenir have nearly all become absorbed in the general population of the town and district. Out of the 376 immigrants who arrived on Tuesday afternoon, there are only about 60[43] remaining in the barrack awaiting engagements yesterday. Amongst this number are about 4 girls, 30 young men, and 15 married couples, most of whom will probably meet with engagements during this the 3rd day of hiring."

Once he had reached his destination William no longer recorded his experiences in a diary, but we know that he married Jessie Brunton Stewart, and remained in Australia for the rest of his life. They had 6 children, including a daughter Mary, a son Robert who died from his wounds in 1917 in France[44] and a son Athol. The family lived at Laurieton and Riverstone.

---

[43] This reduced to 50 the following day, the delay in finding engagements for the rest being blamed on the severe weather conditions.
[44] See appendix

Robert Rankine[45]

---

[45] Courtesy of Riverstone and District Historical Society

Robert RANKINE

Regimental Number	6077
Place of Birth	Laurieton, NSW
School	Various
Religion	Presbyterian
Occupation	Plumber
Address	P/O Riverstone, NSW
Marital Status	Single
Age at Embarkation	25
Next of Kin	Mrs.J.Rankine
Enlistment Date	22/3/1916
Rank on Enlistment	Private
Unit Name	2nd Battalion, 19th Reinforcement
Embarkation Details	Sydney, 22/8/1916 on HMAT A18 Wiltshire
Fate	Died of wounds, April 1917
Place of Death	Hermies, France
Age at Death	26 yrs 6 months
Place of Burial	Pozieres British Cemetery Plot 2, Row J, Grave 21
Panel Number, Roll of Honour Australian War Memorial	34
Parents	William and Jessie Rankine
Other Details	British War & Victory Medals

46

Williams daughter Mary married Raymond Vaughan, and his son Athol married a Miss Grace Parkhill of Westmead and Riverstone. Jessie died in June 1923, less than a year after Marys marriage. In 1925 William sold his house and land at Riverstone and retired to Wentworthville. He died unexpectedly having fallen while mounting a horse at Church Road, Riverstone in December 1929[47].

48

---

[47] Not December 1930 as recorded on his gravestone – a masons 'typo'

[48] Back row: Bill Vaughan, William Rankine , Mary Rankine, Ray Vaughan, William Cruickshank. Front row: Stella Rumery, Irene Harris, Ida Rumery. Photo courtesy of Riverstone and District Historical Society

Following his death, the Windsor and Richmond Gazette published an obituary to William. His remains were interred at the Presbyterian Cemetery on 2nd January 1930, 46 years to the day after his arrival at Maryborough.

Friday 11 January 1930, Windsor and Richmond Gazzete, Page 12

"The Late William Rankine

With the death of Mr. Wm. Rankine on Sunday 30th December, Riverstone lost one of its most popular and highly esteemed residents. Mr.Rankine, at the time of his death was 67 years of age, and arrived at Maryborough, Queensland , from Peebles, Scotland, some 46 years ago. He afterwards moved to Gympie and later to Laurieton, where he married and settled down for a number of years. Subsequently he moved to Crows Nest, and later to the Riverstone District where he had resided for about 25 years. During his residence in Riverstone he left the district for two brief periods, to go to Dorrigo and also Lismore. For the past 12 years he had been associated with the Riverstone Meat Co. and during his employment with that firm had made himself one of the most popular employees of the concern. His keen interest in sport was known to all and particularly his association with cricket, especially international matches. The reason why he displayed such an interest in cricket may have caused many of his friends to wonder, but the secret of his interest may be due to the fact that for some years he captained a strong cricket team in Laurieton.

Deceased was the father of the late Robert Rankine, who was killed on active service on the 10th April 1917, and is survived by his wife[49] and daughter (Mrs.R.E.Vaughan) and his son Athol, who at present is residing at Auburn. To the remaining relatives we extend our heartfelt sympathy. It is intended to hold a memorial service on Sunday 27th instant, at the Presbyterian Church, of which the late Mr. Rankine was a member."

Williams parents Robert and Jane, together with his youngest sister Margaret, were last recorded as living at No 9 Northgate, on the Valuation Roll for the borough of Peebles for 1901/02. The Proprietor for that address was Wm. Weir, as Treasurer, Kilwinning Freemasons.

Jane Rankine

On 7th September 1888 Williams sister Jane (Janet) Rankine married James/Jim Thomson, Williams old friend, at Peebles in Scotland. Shortly afterwards they emigrated to Taree, in New South Wales where James worked as a plumber. They had 4 children, the first 3 were all born at Taree. John was born in 1889; James in 1891; Jean Naomi on 10th January 1894;

---

[49] William Rankines wife had died in 1923. He may have remarried, but this has not been confirmed.

and Catherine (Kit). They returned to Scotland around 1900, living initially at Cathcart, Glasgow. Williams diary was passed to his sister Jane and then to Jean, who in turn passed it on to her son William Smith McInally. Fortunately he passed a photocopy, here transcribed, to his daughter, since shortly after his death the original diary was lost.

Above: William Rankines niece Jean Naomi Thomson, daughter of Jim Thomson, with her son William Smith McInally.

Appendices

1. Index to Passengers

2. William Rankines family tree.

3. The Thomson family tree

4. Extended family: The McInally family tree

INDEX TO PASSENGERS

Surname	First Name		Age
Adie	Alex		21
Agnew	Mary		35
Anderson	Anthony		19
Anderson	Eliza		29
Anderson	James		49
Anderson	Mary		11
Anderson	Rosina	d	7
Anderson	Rosina		48
Avery	Emma		29
Barron	E.S.	b/d	Inf
Barron	Ellen		25
Barron	George		32
Beanland	Joshua		28
Bell	Joseph		27
Bell	Mary		23
Benten	Robert		28
Bird	John		26
Bird	Sarah		20
Bird	Thomas		19
Bishop	Thomas		28
Blanchard	Fred		20
Bonar	Eliza		7

Bonar	Francis	9
Bonar	Hannah	Inf
Bonar	John	4
Bonar	Margaret	12
Bonar	Margaret	36
Bonar	Neil	40
Bonar	Eliza	18
Brambridge	Annie	21
Brinston	James	25
Brown	Ada	6
Brown	Annie	44
Brown	Edith	11
Brown	Florence	1
Brown	Isa	33
Brown	Jessie	3
Brown	John	19
Brown	Joshua	23
Brown	Mary	19
Brown	Martha	8
Brown	Mary	Inf
Brown	Thomas	44
Brown	Wm	21
Browning	Mrs	20
Browning	Agnes	Inf
Browning	John	23
Burke	Mary	22

Burns	John	23
Butler	Bridget	20
Byrne	James	29
Cairns	Andrew	8
Cairns	Catherine	6
Cairns	James	14
Cairns	Jane	6
Cairns	Jane	38
Cairns	Jemina	3
Cairns	Jemina	27
Cairns	John	48
Cairns	Mary	2
Cairns	Mary	Inf
Cairns	Peter	30
Cairns	Robert	8
Cairns	Thomas	2
Cairns	Wm	18
Caldwell	David	9
Caldwell	Francis	16
Caldwell	Helen	12
Caldwell	Jessie	22
Caldwell	Johanna	40
Caldwell	John	20
Caldwell	Joseph	18
Caldwell	Matthew	24
Caldwell	Wm	11

Campbell	Alex	30
Campbell	Colin	26
Canning	Hugh	18
Cardock	Agnes	32
Cardock	Charles	24
Carroll	George	22
Challerton	Alice	8
Challerton	Ann	47
Challerton	Robert	7
Challerton	Sarah	14
Challerton	Thomas	4
Christie	Eliza	20
Christie	Henry	26
Chutterton	Wm	21
Clarkson	Mary	17
Coghlan	Mary	21
Coine	Philip	22
Coman	Bridget	18
Coman	Mary	16
Connolly	Hattie	25
Connolly	Thomas	29
Cooney	Mary	18
Cooper	Alice	15
Cooper	Christina	35
Corr	Bridget	18
Corr	Ellen	16

Corr	Ellen		30
Corr	James		22
Corr	John		26
Corr	John		33
Corr	Pat		24
Corr	Pat		25
Corr	Peter		20
Croft	Ada		7
Croft	Alice		6
Croft	Annie		12
Croft	Charles		13
Croft	Charles		38
Croft	Gertrude		2
Croft	Kate		8
Croft	Lissie		10
Croft	Susan		42
Croft	Willie		4
Crosbie	Isabella		23
Cune	Anne		20
Dainton	Geo		16
Dale	Eliza		18
Dale	Margaret		25
Davidson	Richard	d	28
Dick	Margaret		16
Dick	Mary		6
Dick	Mary		29

Dick	Robert	9
Dick	Thomas	3
Dick	Wm	15
Dick	Wm	38
Dickson	Ann	37
Dickson	George	3
Dickson	Helen	1
Dickson	Robert	42
Dickson	Thomas	6
Dickson	Wm	11
Doig	George	24
Doig	Jessie	22
Duncan	John	19
Dunn	Agnes	1
Dunn	Agnes	24
Dunn	John	24
Elliott	Sarah	19
English	Wm	28
Farrelly	Mary	23
Figgins	Annie	22
Finne	Eliza	20
Fitzsimon	Bernard	23
Fleming	Helen	Inf
Fleming	Janette	31
Fleming	John	12
Fleming	Mary	22

Fleming	Robert		28
Fleming	Robert		Inf
Fleming	Wm		6
Fleming	Wm		36
Fulton	Catherine		24
Fulton	David	d	Inf
Fulton	James		22
Galachai	John		20
Galloway	Alex		5
Galloway	Alex		27
Galloway	Mary		28
Galloway	Robert		Inf
Galloway	Wm		2
Genn	Henry		16
Genn	Herbert		1
Genn	Sarah		26
Genn	Wm		26
Godfrey	Ann		29
Godfrey	Helen		40
Godfrey	Maggie		15
Godfrey	Robert		19
Graham	Mary		22
Grant	Alex		22
Greenholdby	Ben		24
Greghegson	Timothy		22
Gregory	Robert		21

Greig	Wm		22
Grendenning	Mary		19
Groombridge	Kate		21
Hall	Joe		20
Hawksworth	Ed		24
Henderson	Alex		18
Hickey	Mark		24
Houston	George		17
Howie	Eliza		22
Hunter	Isabella		22
Ireland	Jessie		18
Isbestor	James F		21
Isbestor	James		17
Jenkins	Morgan		25
Johnstone	Lizzie		26
Kelly	Honora		26
Kelly	Mary		17
Kennedy	Wm		21
Killeen	Bridget		20
Kinney	Bernard		25
Kinney	Bridget		26
Kinney	Pat		4
Kirkland	Robert		20
Kitchings	Adam		7
Kitchings	Alex	d	Inf
Kitchings	Joan		3

Kitchings	Joseph	8
Kitchings	Joseph	30
Kitchings	Lillian	26
Kitchings	Mary	5
Lappin	James	39
Lappin	John	6
Lappin	Mary	Inf
Lappin	Sarah	35
Lappin	Wm	5
Leak	Margaret	26
Lee	Archie	21
Leighton	James	23
Lewis	Ben	26
Lewis	John	21
Liddell	Wm	22
Leisham	Harriet	23
Livingstone	Agnes	27
Livingstone	Donald	10
Livingstone	Donald	29
Livingstone	Martha	2
Marlow	Ellen	18
Mathewson	Isabella	23
Mathewson	Joseph	26
Mathewson	Joseph	Inf
McAra	Daniel	28
McCann	Mary	19

McDonald	D	22
McDonald	Hugh	22
McEwan	Henry	4
McEwan	John	6
McEwan	John	31
McEwan	Mary	35
McEwan	Mary	35
McGorrie	Eliza	28
McKean	Annie	18
McKenzie	Alex	23
McKenzie	Eliza	21
McKenzie	Kenneth	27
McKenzie	Murdo	22
McKenzie	Wm	22
McKilcher	Duncan	24
McLean	H.	22
McLean	John	28
McLeod	John	27
McLoughlin	Mary	21
McMilligan	John	23
McVillie	Jane	16
Mercer	Robert	23
Morris	Fanny	22
Mour	George	23
Muir	Thomas	29
Munro	Andrune	20

Murison	Ann		17
Murison	Ann		37
Murison	Charlotte	d	Inf
Murison	David		7
Murison	Eliza		17
Murison	Harriet		11
Murison	John		13
Murison	Nathaniel		53
Murison	Robert		1
Murphy	Bridget		20
Murray	Jane		27
Murray	Robert		27
Nicol	Wm		22
Neilson	James		24
Owen	Catherine		8
Owen	Jane		38
Owen	Margaret		3
Owen	Rosie ?		1
Owen	Wm		30
Owen	Wm		Inf
Pallistein	Eliza		11
Pallistein	George		1
Pallistein	Hannah		36
Pallistein	Isabella	b	Inf
Pallistein	James		6
Pallistein	Thomas		4

Pallistein	Thomas	39
Palmer	Arthur	20
Phillips	Claretta	19
Phillips	Shinclair ?	26
Potter	Isabella	23
Potter	Robert	1
Potter	Robert	21
Praddle	Doctor	
Preddy	James	24
Preston	Alex	20
Pritchard	Thomas	22
Quane	Bridget	19
Quane	Mary	28
Ramsey	James	22
Rankine	Wm	20
Reaney	Eliza	32
Reaney	Harry	4
Reaney	Jessie	2
Reaney	John	38
Reaney	Lewis McD b	Inf
Reaney	Thomas	7
Robb	John	26
Robertson	Ann	15
Robertson	Crawford	1
Robertson	James	24
Robertson	Jessie	23

Robertson	John		22
Robertson	Maggie		2
Robertson	Wm		26
Robinson	Arthur		21
Robinson	David		19
Rourke	Maria		18
Rourke	Michael		20
Sanderson	Mary		17
Sexton	Annie		19
Sheen	Fanny		19
Simmons	Mrs		50
Simmons, Mrs	Matron		
Simpson	Jessie	d	1
Simpson	Mary		28
Simpson	Thomas		26
Smith	Anna		14
Smith	Charles		21
Smith	Helen		19
Smith	John		24
Smith	Mary		18
Smith	Myra		17
Stephenson	Wm		20
Stewart	David		26
Stewart	John		22
Stewart	Josephine		Inf
Stewart	Mary		25

Sterling,Cpt	Robert	
Tilford	Wm	28
Tait	Alex	2
Tait	Alex	29
Tait	Catherine	26
Tait	Catherine	3
Tait	James	Inf
Tait	Wm	6
Ulett	Alice	17
Ulett	Edith	8
Ulett	Edwin	16
Ulett	Emily	14
Ulett	Fanny	38
Ulett	Flo	6
Ulett	James	10
Ulett	James	49
Walker	Betsey	43
Walker	Ellen	16
Walker	George	8
Walker	J.J.	13
Walker	Wm	11
Walker	Wm	45
Ward	Christina	23
Webster	Clara	15
West	James	19
White	Emma	21

White	Jane	Inf
White	John	23
Wilson	Annie	19
Wilson	David	1
Wilson	Eliza	7
Wilson	James	8
Wilson	James	18
Wilson	James	25
Wilson	Mary	28
Wilson	Robert	4
Wilson	Robert	33
Wright	Naomi	23
Young	Agnes	28
Young	Allen	20
Young	Christine	5
Young	David	3
Young	James	29
Yourk	Catherine	23
Yourk	Pat	25

Note: b/d – Born / Died on Board

The Rankine Family Tree

William Rankine = Margaret Scott
1770   1776

William Rankine = Margaret Rough
b. 1801   b. 1804

John   Alison James   William Mary Isbel   Robert = Jane Melrose
1836   1826   1826   1826   1827 1830   1829   1837

John Melrose = Jane Hogg
1777 - 1849

James Melrose = Jane Whey
1812 - 1861   1815

Janet   James   Robert   Charles   John   Margaret William   =   Jessie Stewart
1863 - 1940 1866   1869   1871   1874   1876   1861   1869

David Stewart

Ray =   Mary   Robert   Athol = Grace
Vaughan   Parkhill

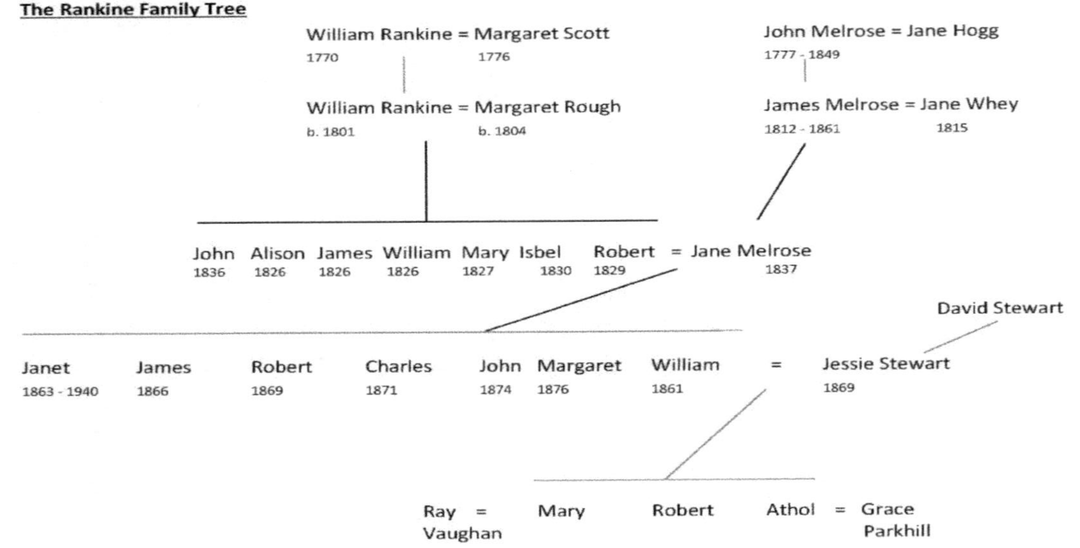

50

The Thomson Family Tree

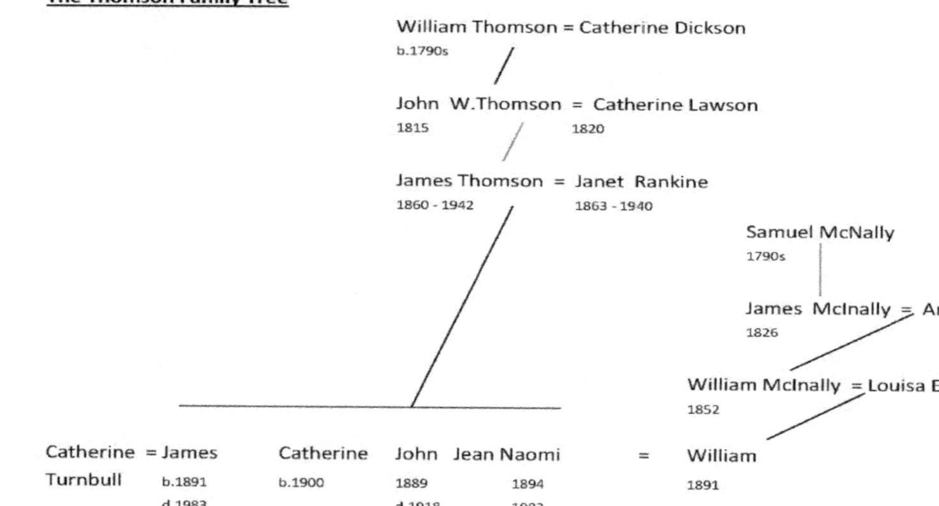

The McInallys

A1) Samuel McNally, Farmer, Tynan, County Armagh, Ireland, m. unknown

  B1) James McNally b.1826, d.1902 Cathcart, Scotland m. Anne, daughter of Alexander Tate at Middletown, Armagh, on 16th October 1851

    C1) Samuel d.in infancy

    C2) James McNally, b.circa 1851 Armagh died Chicago. Married unknown, had issue.

    C3) William b.1852 d.30.9.1906 married Louisa Emily Smith b.1856, d.22.3.1919

      i.   Ellen Jane (Nellie) b.20.12.1876 d.13.12.1937 m. Andrew Reid

        a) Louisa Emily m. John Roberts

          i. George Iain m.1 Maisie, m.2 cousin May (see below)

            a) Fiona

            b) Angus

            c) Jane

        b) Charlotte (Lottie) m. Joseph Halbert

          i. Douglas m. ?

      ii.   Annie b.30.1.1879 d.18.4.1961 m. Robert Thomson

      iii. Margaret b.14.2.1881 m. George Campbell

        a) Pearl m. Rowland Moose, they had 3 children.

        b) Ruby m. Jack

          i.   Betty

          ii.   Nancy

      iv. Louisa Emily (Amy) b.11.2.1883 d.feb 1959 m. Oscar J.Ottis

      v.   Elizabeth b.1886 d.12.6.1897 d.aged 11

      vi. James b.16.3.1888 d.22.5.1941 m.Pearl

      vii. Mary Alice b.25.1.1891 d.aged 3 (a wall fell on her)

      viii. William b.25.1.1891 d.16.5.1947 m. **Jean Naomi Thomson b.10.5.1894, d.4.8.1983**

          i.   William Smith b.14.5.22 m. Catherine MacWilliam b.21.12.20

            a) Iain James p.Monica Moro

              i.William

              ii.Toby

            b) Christine Anne m.Pat Cronin

              i.Aidan

              ii.Grace

              iii.Eleanor

          ii.   Jean Catherine May b.16.2.28 m.Q2 1954 James S. Allan MacColl

            a) Carolyn m. David Reid

              i. James

              ii.Victoria

              iii. Rory

              iv. Emily

            b) Kevin m. Wendy

              i. Cameron

      ix. Violet b.30.8.1896 m.1 Crawford (divorced) m.2 Fisher, m.3 Howard Dabney

          i.   William m. Carol

            a) Reid

            b) Neal

    C4) Ann Jane b.c 1856 d.27.9.1884

    C5) Margaret b.c 1860 d.4.1.1896

    C6) John b.c 1863 d.9.2.1885

    C7) Elizabeth b.17/11/1865, Tynan, Armagh, d.18.11.1893